DEVOTIONS
FOR BECOMING A

Beautiful
Woman of
God

Published by Barbour Publishing, Inc., 1810 Barbour Drive, Uhrichsville, Ohio 44683, www.barbourbooks.com

Our mission is to inspire the world with the life-changing message of the Bible.

Member of the
Evangelical Christian
Publishers Association

Printed in the United States of America.

DEVOTIONS
FOR BECOMING A

Beautiful
Woman of
God

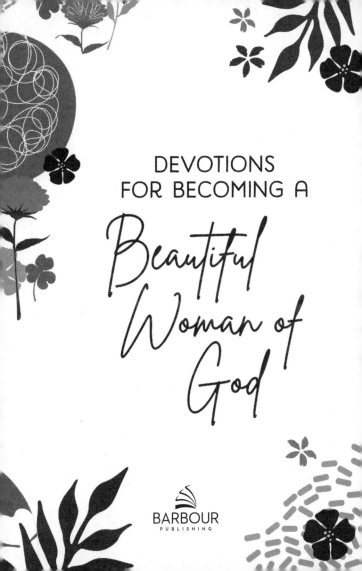

BARBOUR
PUBLISHING

INTRODUCTION

*I praise you because I am fearfully
and wonderfully made; your works
are wonderful, I know that full well.*

PSALM 139:14 NIV

We women are some of God's most amazingly diverse creations. From our gifts and talents to our insecurities and hang-ups, our heavenly Father wants us to know how truly wonderful He made us—that He cherishes us—that He loves us unconditionally—and that He desires a closer relationship with us.

In these pages you'll find the encouragement you need as you strive to live a life that is firmly rooted in the loving adoration of the Father. You are—and will always be—wonderfully made!

A BEAUTIFUL AROMA

*God thinks of us as a perfume that brings
Christ to everyone. For people who are
being saved, this perfume has a sweet
smell and leads them to a better life.*

2 CORINTHIANS 2:15-16 CEV

She breezed in and sat down in front of me
at an Indiana University basketball game
on that cold February night. She was an older
woman, dressed in a navy business suit, with
a red-and-white scarf tied stylishly around her
neck. Her silver hair was neatly tucked behind
her ears in a classic bob, and her lipstick was a
perfect IU crimson color.

I would have guessed her to be in her early
fifties—probably an IU professor. As she settled into her seat, a wonderful aroma filled the
air. It broke through the smells of stale popcorn

and overcooked hot dogs and filled my nostrils. I inhaled deeply and said, "Mmmm."

"Do you smell that?" I whispered to my mother.

"Yes, it's marvelous," she answered.

There was no doubt. The wonderful aroma had wafted in with the classy lady in front of us. As the halftime buzzer sounded, I leaned forward and tapped the woman on her shoulder.

"Excuse me, ma'am. You smell so wonderful. Could you tell me what you're wearing?"

"Thank you," she said, then told me the name of her perfume.

I shared the information with my mother, and we each made a mental note about our next perfume purchase. I wanted to smell just like the classy lady with the silver hair.

You know, the Bible says we are the aroma of Christ. When we enter a room, we should carry His fragrance with us. His aroma should be so pleasing on us that people will tap us on the shoulder and ask, "Excuse me, ma'am. You smell wonderful. What are you wearing?" With that opening, we can share Jesus Christ with every person who notices our Christlike aroma.

Maybe your fragrance smells more like those overcooked weenies or stale popcorn. If so, you just need a "smell makeover." Ask God to replace your human smell with His divine fragrance so that you will be a witness of His sweetness everywhere you go. Ask the Lord to fill you with His fragrant love so that it enters the room even before you do. He will. He doesn't want His children to go around smelling stinky. After all, we are the aroma of Christ, and that's better than the finest perfume. (MMA)

GOD REJOICES IN YOUR CONFIDENCE

*I rejoice therefore that I have
confidence in you in all things.*

2 CORINTHIANS 7:16 KJV

*B*ut God wants you to have confidence!"
Those words echoed in my head as I tried
not to hyperventilate. Stage fright was making
my palms sweat and my knees quiver. Waiting
to be introduced, I fought to stay calm, remem-
bering those words of support from a woman
in my church. I loved Ann dearly, and she had
been a spiritual mentor—and mother—to me.
When I'd been invited to speak for the first time
at a church, I had sought her out.

"I don't know if I can do this. Even the thought
of standing in front of all those people does all
kinds of weird stuff to my body."

Ann laughed. "But this is a gift, an opportunity from God to give your testimony, to tell those folks what He's done in your life. You can't turn your back on that."

"What kind of testimony will it be if I make a fool out of myself?"

"You won't. Pray about it. He gave you the story, led you to live it. He'll certainly give you the confidence to share it. Remember what Paul wrote to the Corinthians, once they'd straightened themselves out and were back on the right road. They'd gained confidence in their faith, and Paul rejoiced in that." She hugged me. "God wants you to be confident!"

I took another deep breath and let it out slowly as I heard the hostess winding up her introduction. "Okay, God," I whispered, "let's get me through this, and we'll both rejoice." I stepped up, thanked the hostess, and gripped the sides of the podium as if it were going to flee from the room. My voice trembled, but as my message

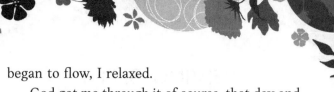

began to flow, I relaxed.

God got me through it of course, that day and many times since, mostly because Ann's words made an impact that has never lessened. God wants us to be confident—in our faith, in our gifts, and especially in Him, and He rejoices when our trust in Him gives us the confidence to tackle whatever challenge He puts before us. (RR)

GIVING BIRTH

"Do not fear what they fear,
and do not dread it."

ISAIAH 8:12 NIV

Go to any baby shower, and sooner or later the birthing stories start. Comparisons run the gamut from the most nervous husband to the longest labor. I'm personally intrigued by the unusual places infants choose to be born, giving little thought to their mothers' inconvenience or modesty.

My aunt June birthed one of her children in the elevator on the way up to the hospital delivery room. Pat's husband was adamant that his wife not deliver their child in his new Cadillac. (They couldn't make it to the hospital in time.) So Pat delivered their bundle of joy on their kitchen table. Grace's story may top both Pat's and June's.

Grace and her husband, Bill, were "bush" missionaries in Indonesia decades ago. Their second daughter was born in their lodging with Bill as the delivering doctor. Bill wasn't a physician, a nurse, an EMT, or a paramedic. There was no 911 in those days, least of all in the jungle. But Bill "read up" on delivering a baby. When the time came, he and Grace and their little newborn just did it.

What amazes me about these three women and their colorful stories is their lack of panic in their situations. Each one decided she would simply do what it had come time to do—push! June and Pat didn't plan their unorthodox deliveries, but Grace did. Most of us would fear delivering a child miles from any kind of medical help or facility. Our comfort is tied to the familiar—to the known standard of care. Grace's peace was tied to her God. She was confident that she and her husband were doing what God had called them to do and were where He had called them to do it. When her delivery date arrived, she had spent a lot of time in preparatory prayer. She was ready.

Grace is now in her nineties and has had many difficult moments in recent months. Bill's Alzheimer's has taken him from her in many ways. Grace's health fails too. She had to have a leg amputated. As I talked with her one evening, she rubbed the leg that now ends at her knee.

"I never thought this would happen to. . .," she started. She sniffed back her threatening tears and held up her head. "God is faithful. He's taking care of me. We'll get through this together." Grace has never been one to indulge in self-pity—not when she was delivering a baby in the jungle and not when she lost a limb. Her serenity is no secret. Her "LORD is a God who knows" (1 Samuel 2:3 NIV), and she is content. (KAD)

PINK PROMISES

*I am sure that nothing can separate us
from God's love—not life or death, not angels
or spirits, not the present or the future.*

ROMANS 8:38 CEV

*A*fter my father died, my sister and I helped our mom go through his personal items. I couldn't wait to get into Daddy's special drawer— it was the one drawer in his nightstand that he kept off limits to us kids. I remember once trying to ease open the drawer to sneak some quarters from his big bowl of change (I wanted to feed the Pac-Man game at the local arcade), but as I started to reach my hand inside, I heard Dad's voice: "Michelle Leigh Medlock, get out of my drawer!" He didn't mind giving me money for Pac-Man; he just didn't want me in his special drawer.

For years I wondered what could possibly be in that forbidden treasure trove. Why was he so protective of it? Now I would finally know. As I searched through Daddy's things, I found very ordinary items. His comb. Fingernail clippers. His money clip. Pictures of the family. Lots of change. His special calculator he used in business. And a lockbox. When we opened it, we found important documents like his and my mother's marriage license, birth certificates, and the hospital bracelets for all three of us kids—two tiny pink ones and one small blue one. The wording had yellowed over the years, but I could still read "Medlock Girl" and my birth date on one. I held that tiny pink bracelet close to my heart for what seemed like hours. At that moment, I realized how very much my daddy cherished me. He loved me so much that he even treasured my baby bracelet.

Today I keep that baby bracelet in a secret compartment of my purse as a reminder of how much Daddy cared. You may not have a loving earthly father. Or maybe you don't even know your father. But I have good news: you have a heavenly Father who treasures you, and He has little pink bracelets—His promises of love—all throughout His Word. Every time you find one (like Jeremiah 31:3 [NLT], which says, "I have loved you, my people, with an everlasting love"), you will want to hold it close to your heart—just like I did. Spend some time today discovering how much your heavenly Father loves you. It will fill your heart with real joy that will last a lifetime. (MMA)

THE MOST BEAUTIFUL WOMAN IN THE WORLD

*They saw that his face was radiant. Then
Moses would put the veil back over his face
until he went in to speak with the LORD.*

EXODUS 34:35 NIV

*F*ilm legend Audrey Hepburn was named the
most naturally beautiful woman of all time
by a panel of experts in June 2004. Hepburn,
the star of *Roman Holiday* and *Breakfast at Tiffany's*, topped the poll of beauty editors, makeup
artists, fashion editors, model agencies, and fashion
photographers who were asked to choose their
top ten beauties from a list of one hundred.

The women were chosen for their "embodiment of natural beauty, healthy living, *beautiful
on the inside and out*, with great skin and a natural glow to their personality, as well as their

complexion." The article went on to say that Audrey Hepburn is the personification of natural beauty because "she has a rare charm and *inner beauty* that radiates when she smiles. Her skin looks fresh in all her films and her personality really shines through as someone warm and lively."

Wow, that's quite a tribute, huh? Wouldn't it be great to make the Top 100 Beautiful Women of All Time list—let alone be voted number one? But did you notice that Audrey Hepburn's inner beauty was mentioned twice in the judges' reasoning for choosing her? Sure, there were many other beauties who made the list—Marilyn Monroe, Cleopatra. Some may have been even more beautiful than Hepburn, but apparently their inner beauty was found lacking, even though their exterior beauty was striking.

That's good news, isn't it? That means even if our skin isn't flawless, even if our teeth aren't perfectly straight, and even if our hair has more bad days than good ones, we can still "radiate beauty" because of our gorgeous inner looks. In other words, if your heart is filled with the love of Jesus, that is going to cause you to glow. Did you know that Moses had to cover his face after he had spent time in God's presence because his face actually glowed? It's true!

Spend some time with God today, and get a makeover by the Master. Soon you'll radiate His love, and people will find you attractive. You might even say, "You'll glow, girl!" (MMA)

WHAT'S HOLDING YOU BACK?

Thank you for making me so wonderfully complex! Your workmanship is marvelous—how well I know it.

PSALM 139:14 NLT

*F*anny Crosby, the author of more than nine thousand hymns and one thousand secular poems and songs, never let her physical challenges stop the call she felt on her life. And she never let her disability become a hindrance in her relationship with God.

Born in 1820, Fanny had her vision at birth. But at six weeks, she suffered an eye inflammation. The family's usual doctor wasn't available, so they sought help from a man who claimed to be medically qualified to help. He put a poultice on Fanny's eyes, leaving the infant's eyes scarred.

The "doctor" left town—and Fanny blind.

Growing up blind wasn't easy, but Fanny didn't blame God for her situation. She didn't ask, "Why me?" Instead, she determined in her heart to make a difference in this world. She expressed that desire in her first poem:

O what a happy soul am I!
Although I cannot see,
I am resolved that in this world,
Contented I will be.
How many blessings I enjoy,
That other people don't.
To weep and sigh because I'm blind,
I cannot and I won't!

When adversity happens in life, people respond in different ways. Some give up. Some get angry with God. And some become even more determined to reach their goals and dreams—like Fanny. Without her songs "Safe in the Arms of

Jesus," "Pass Me Not, O Gentle Savior," "Blessed Assurance," and so many others, our world would not be the same.

So here's my question to you: What are you letting hold you back? If you've been dealing with a painful disability or been emotionally crippled due to circumstances beyond your control, God cares. He knows you're hurting. But He wants to give you beauty for ashes. He wants you to know that His plans for you have been in existence since before the foundations of the earth. Despite your troubles, God's plan for you has never changed, and His plan is a good one!

If you don't know the plan that God has for you, ask Him to show you. Tell Him that you are ready to carry out all that He has for you to do. Like Fanny, you are an important part of His overall plan in this world. So go ahead. Walk in that plan. (MMA)

A WEIGHTY ISSUE

*If any of you lacks wisdom, you should ask
God, who gives generously to all without
finding fault, and it will be given to you.*

JAMES 1:5 NIV

Standing in line at the supermarket, you can't help noticing the various women's magazines with headlines such as LOSE 10 POUNDS IN 10 DAYS!, WALK YOUR WAY TO A HEALTHY WEIGHT!, and LOSE THOSE LAST FIVE POUNDS EATING TOFU!

If you're like me, you probably buy several of those magazines each month and try eating tofu for a few days until you give in and have a package of M&M's.

With each decade, managing your weight becomes more difficult. Our metabolisms slow down if we're not working out regularly, and the weight slowly acquires on our midsections, hips, and thighs. Ugh! If your "fat jeans" fit perfectly today, then you're not alone. According to the American Obesity Organization, more than half of adult US women are overweight, and more than one-third are obese. Obviously, we have some work to do in this area. But here's the good news: we don't have to do that work alone.

God cares about every little thing that affects our lives—including those extra five, ten, or twenty pounds that are hanging on for dear life! Let Him help you to achieve your ideal weight. Ask Him to get involved in your quest for fitness and a healthy lifestyle.

My pastor's wife had struggled with her weight off and on for years, and then she finally got a plan. No, it wasn't Weight Watchers, LA Weight Loss, or Jenny Craig. It was God's plan! She said that she prayed about her weight issue, and God impressed upon her to do three things: drink more water than soft drinks, quit eating after 6:00 p.m., and walk two miles three days a week. Those instructions didn't seem that hard, so she started following them. Twenty pounds lighter now, she is a happier, healthier woman. The plan God gave my pastor's wife may not be a perfect plan for you, but rest assured, God has a weight-loss plan with your name on it. Just ask for His wisdom today, and leave those supermarket magazines on the racks. Who likes tofu, anyway? (MMA)

TO FOLLOW GOD'S CALL

And Deborah, a prophetess, the wife of
Lapidoth, she judged Israel at that time.

JUDGES 4:4 KJV

Throughout scripture, the faith that women have
in God provides them with the confidence
to stand up for their beliefs, face down armies,
and deal with the pressures of their lives. One
woman is even called to guide ten thousand men
into battle.

The only woman to sit as a judge over Israel,
Deborah's most vital relationships are introduced
in this first mention of her. The prophets in Old
Testament times were men and women called by
God to communicate His will to the people. Thus,
Deborah already had a strong relationship with
the Lord when she was called to sit as judge for
Israel at a time of harsh oppression. She was also

a wife, with an established household and place in her world. Yet in a society that did not always value women as leaders, she answered God's call on her life.

Using her wisdom to settle disputes for her people, however, is a far cry from leading them into battle against an army featuring nine hundred iron chariots, vehicles that had revolutionized warfare and forced the Israelites to seek refuge in fortified cities. Jabin, the king in Canaan, had dealt harshly with the Israelites for more than twenty years, using his army to keep them under his rule. Finally, they cried out to God for relief in what appeared to be an impossible situation to overcome.

Deborah, however, had the ability to see beyond the current situation. She was a woman of vision, and she called on Barak to do as the Lord had commanded, to take his troops and prepare to face Sisera, Jabin's general, in a battle to save their people. Barak's response—that he would do so only if she was with him (see Judges 4:8)—underscores the trust Israel had placed in the woman God had called for them.

God always looks for women who are ready to embrace His vision for their lives, their families, and even their nations. Such women of vision have the courage that enables them to conquer and overcome in situations that would otherwise seem unconquerable. (RR)

HERE COMES THE JUDGE

I can do all this through him
who gives me strength.

PHILIPPIANS 4:13 NIV

Do you ever worry about what others think of you? I've found that most women struggle with this issue of being judged—even gorgeous, "got it all together" women. One of my dearest friends is absolutely beautiful. Would you believe that even she worries what others think of her? I once heard her say, "I'd love to do more teaching, but I'm just not ready."

I started thinking, *Wow, if she's not ready, nobody is ready. I've never met anyone who studies the Word of God more than she does.* So I said, "You are *so* ready. You probably have more of God's Word on the inside of you than anyone else I know." With that, she lowered her head and sighed. I had

touched on something that upset her.

"What's the problem?" I pushed.

"Well, I have to lose at least fifteen more pounds before I'll be ready. I worry that everyone will be looking at how big my behind is rather than focusing on the message God's given me to speak."

I couldn't believe my ears. The devil had so deceived her. She had become so worried about what others would think of her that she wasn't walking in the fullness of God. She wasn't allowing herself to be used by Him.

As I drove home that day, I began to think back on all of the times I'd allowed my worries to keep me from serving God. I thought about specific instances when I'd been so afraid of being judged by others that I had completely missed an opportunity to serve Him. It made me sad—not just for me, but for all of my sisters in Christ who had done the same thing.

Are you one of those sisters? Have you been

allowing your insecurities and fear of being judged to keep you from doing great things for God? If so, don't be sad. Just give those concerns to God, and ask Him to fill you up with His love and confidence. Remind yourself throughout the day that you can do all things through Christ who gives you strength, and then go forward and change the world. You have much to offer! (MMA)

GET A JOY INFUSION

"Don't be dejected and sad, for the
joy of the LORD is your strength!"

NEHEMIAH 8:10 NLT

The Word tells us that the devil comes to steal and destroy (John 10:10)—and one of the things he loves to take from Christians is their joy. Do you know why? Because the joy of the Lord is our strength, and the devil knows that truth. He will do everything he can to take that strength from us.

That is why you have to be aware of the devil's crafty schemes for stealing your joy. For instance, if going to the congested grocery store on Saturday afternoon steals your joy, go shopping on a weekday evening or ask your spouse to make the Saturday run. If driving in rush-hour traffic stresses you out and steals your joy, try avoiding the crush by working out after quitting time and driving home later when the traffic has thinned. Or if you must drive at that crazy time of day, listen to praise and worship music while sitting in traffic.

You can do other things to help keep your joy at an optimum level as well. Make sure you get enough sleep each night. Exercise on a regular basis. Eat a nutritionally balanced diet. Drink plenty of water. Don't overload your schedule with too many activities, which can lead to stress. Surround yourself with positive people. Finally, make time to laugh each day.

Ask God to give you a daily infusion of joy. Keep your heart and head full of the Word of God. Meditate on scriptures that deal with joy, like the following:

- "You brought me more happiness than a rich harvest of grain and grapes" (Psalm 4:7 CEV).

- "You make known to me the path of life; you will fill me with joy in your presence, with eternal pleasures at your right hand" (Psalm 16:11 NIV).

- "Restore to me the joy of your salvation and grant me a willing spirit, to sustain me" (Psalm 51:12 NIV).

God has an endless supply of joy awaiting you, and the devil can't steal it unless you let him. So keep hold of your joy—and refill your supply often. (MMA)

ADOPTION

For God so loved the world that he gave his one and only Son, that whoever believes in him shall not perish but have eternal life.

JOHN 3:16 NIV

*C*hildbirth doesn't conjure up images of serenity for anyone. Especially not for the mother-to-be. Jennifer loves to tell the story of her son's birth. Unable to have children, Jennifer and her husband opted for a private adoption. Over the months of the pregnancy, they got to know the teenage birth mother well. When the actual date of delivery came, however, things did not go well. The mother had a prolonged labor, and the baby was face up. Forceps had to be used, and the special-care nursery team was called in to resuscitate the blue, depressed newborn. His late but lusty cry was music to the ears of his mother.

As one of the team members brought the howling, now pink, infant back to the bedside, the obstetrician asked the exhausted patient he was stitching up one question.

"What's this big ten-pounder's name?"

With a voice weary from her task, but just as resolute, the young woman locked eyes with Jennifer.

"You'll have to ask his mother."

In that moment, holding Joshua in her arms for the first time, Jennifer wept tears of relief and joy. The years have not diminished the memory of the birth mother's loving act of selflessness that gave Jennifer her only son. Peace replaced the hours of anxiety and fear.

How like God's unselfish love for us. God did not give His Son, Jesus Christ, to us or for us as we waited in eager expectation. Rather, He did for us what we could not do for ourselves. Just as Joshua's birth mother gave him to a woman powerless to birth her own son, God gave us His

Son, Jesus Christ, when we were powerless to become members of His family (see Romans 5:6; Galatians 4:4–5).

Jennifer had to receive Joshua to be a mother. We must receive Jesus Christ to be Christians. The Bible tells us, "Just as you received Christ Jesus as Lord, continue to live your lives in him, rooted and built up in him. . .overflowing with thankfulness" (Colossians 2:6–7 NIV). That's how we secure our relationship with God. And, oddly enough, it's called. . ."adoption" (Ephesians 1:5 KJV). (KAD)

WORDS OF WISDOM FROM ELEANOR ROOSEVELT

As God's chosen people, holy and dearly loved, clothe yourselves with compassion, kindness, humility, gentleness and patience.

COLOSSIANS 3:12 NIV

*E*leanor Roosevelt has been called the most revered woman of her generation. She made a difference every place she ever dwelled. She not only gave birth to six children, but she also served as a dynamic political helpmate to her husband, Franklin Delano Roosevelt.

Eleanor Roosevelt literally transformed the role of First Lady, holding press conferences, traveling to all parts of the country, giving lectures and radio broadcasts, and expressing her opinions in a daily syndicated newspaper column called "My Day." You might say that she was a spitfire, a woman on a mission, a servant to humankind, a loving wife and mother, and a role model for all women.

Knowing of her accomplishments, I was very interested to discover Mrs. Roosevelt had been a very shy and awkward child. Her mother died when she was only eight years old, and her father died just two years later. It wasn't until she began attending a distinguished school in England that she began to develop self-confidence. During that self-discovery phase, she wrote, "No matter how plain a woman may be, if truth and loyalty are stamped upon her face, all will be attracted to her."

What wise words from such a young teen, huh? If only we all understood that truth. For years, society has told us that if we're not beautiful—like the cover girls on magazines—then we have no place in this world. Many women feel they don't have a voice because they don't fit into a size 6 suit. Many of us have bought the

lie. But no more!

Like Eleanor Roosevelt, we too can overcome our shyness and change our world. Have you ever met someone who isn't really that physically attractive, but after you're around that person for any length of time, you see her as lovely? That's the same quality Eleanor Roosevelt understood. She got it! It's not what's on the outside that makes us worthy, lovely, and attractive. That kind of beauty is fleeting. It's that loyalty, truth, and love on the inside of us, spilling out onto others, that draws people to us. In other words, it's the Jesus in us that makes us irresistible.

If you're feeling plain, unworthy, unattractive, and unnoticed—give yourself a makeover from the inside out. Ask God to develop the fruits of the Spirit within you, and allow the Lord to fill you with His love. Pretty soon, you'll be confident and irresistible—just like Eleanor Roosevelt. And you'll make a difference every place you go! (MMA)

THERE IS NO *I* IN *TEAM*

*Just as a body, though one, has many
parts, but all its many parts form
one body, so it is with Christ.*

1 CORINTHIANS 12:12 NIV

Is your nickname "Tammy Takeover"? Do you
try to do everything alone? If so, we should
form a support group—because I also struggle
with that I'll-just-do-it-myself attitude.

Of course, that line of thinking isn't original.
The world has been telling us for years, "If you
want something done right, you have to do it
yourself." So I decided I would. I tried to do
it all—all by myself—all the time. I ended up
overwrought, stressed, and mean. (Yes, just ask
my husband. I so didn't have the joy of the Lord
in my life.)

God didn't intend for us to go it alone. He

even addresses that errant line of thinking in 1 Corinthians 12:12, using the human body as an example of teamwork. We are just one part of the big picture. We each play an important role, but we will never accomplish what God has for us if we try to do everything all alone. Why? Look to the verse for the answer: according to God's Word, we are just one part of the body. No matter what a great eyeball you are, you will never be able to hear, because you're not an ear!

So quit trying to be an ear! Be the best eye-ball you can be, and work with the person in your life who was called to be an ear. Together, you will do much! Alone, you will just be a good eye—nothing more.

Teamwork, whether you are in an office setting or helping with vacation Bible school, is vitally important. Lose the "Tammy Takeover" mentality and do your part with the rest of the body, and big things can be accomplished in a short time. And the really great part is that you will be much happier! You will get to enjoy the experience and celebrate with the team members when "all of y'all" (Texan plural for "y'all") meet your goal! It's a win-win situation.

So go out and do your part, but don't try to do everyone else's part too. If you feel yourself moving into the I-can-do-it-all-by-myself mode, ask God to keep you focused on what He has called you to do and nothing more. Remember, there is no *I* in *TEAM*—but there are great rewards and happiness when we choose to work as a team. (MMA)

YOU'VE GOT IT
ALL WRONG

And the servant of the Lord must not strive;
but be gentle unto all men, apt to teach, patient.

2 TIMOTHY 2:24 KJV

*P*riscilla of the infant Christian church appears in four books of the New Testament. Her résumé, impressive even by today's standards, sounds like that of a contemporary woman. She and her husband had their own business, moved frequently, and had to adapt to life on the go—not always by choice (see Acts 18:2). They were teachers, hosts of house churches, and risk takers. Paul tells us they "laid down their own necks" to save his (Romans 16:4 KJV). Every sentence about Priscilla invites speculation about this fascinating woman. It's been suggested that since her name almost always precedes her husband's in the Bible, she was probably the more notable of the couple.

When an erudite man named Apollos came on the scene preaching about Jesus, Priscilla and her husband were there. "He was a learned man, with a thorough knowledge of the Scriptures. . . . He spoke with great fervor and taught about Jesus accurately, though he knew only the baptism of John" (Acts 18:24–25 NIV). With characteristic simplicity, Luke, the writer of Acts, sets the stage for some potential problems in this new organism called the Christian church. An unknown had come into the synagogue at Ephesus preaching "with great fervor" but telling only half the story. Do Priscilla and her husband get upset? Do they take this newbie to task? Do they get rattled and start to shout down the visiting teacher? Not according to the Word.

"When Priscilla and Aquila heard him, they invited him to their home and explained to him the way of God more adequately" (Acts 18:26 NIV).

No strong-arming; no heated, public exchange.

Priscilla and Aquila heard their fellow believer out, gave him the benefit of the doubt, and then gently instructed him. They recognized their soul mate in the spread of the Gospel—to the mutual benefit of all. (Check out the rest of Acts 18.)

What a demonstration of correcting a misguided, overzealous new Christian. Priscilla's calm serenity in sharing the rest of the story with Apollos is a lesson for all of us. More is accomplished with gentle instruction than by badgering or embarrassing the less-informed or immature believer. Softening correction with genuine encouragement works not only in the church but also at work and in the home. (KAD)

"YOU LOOK MAHVELOUS!"

Thank you for making me so wonderfully complex! Your workmanship is marvelous—how well I know it.

PSALM 139:14 NLT

I have a friend named Mary whose favorite saying is "You look mahvelous!" This gal knows how to give a compliment. No one can say it quite like Mary. You may not know Mary, but I bet you remember the character Billy Crystal made famous on *Saturday Night Live* by saying, "You look mahvelous!" (In the 1980s, he even had a song titled "You Look Mahvelous!" that played on radios across the United States.)

I've always loved that saying. It's better than just saying, "Hey, you look all right." It's much more exciting to hear, "You look mahvelous!" After fourteen years of marriage, my husband knows which answers will get him into trouble.

For instance, if I ask, "Does this outfit make me look fat?" his answer had better be "No. Are you kidding? How could anything ever make you look fat?" And if I ask, "How do I look?" he'd better not say, "You look okay" or "You look fine." Why? Because *okay* and *fine* translate into *adequate* or *you'll do*. No woman wants to feel like she's just "okay." Women want to look and feel marvelous, right?

Well, in the real world, we often don't feel like we look marvelous. In fact, we may not feel like we even measure up to okay or fine. Am I right? Maybe you were raised in a home where praise was rarely given, so you're not used to hearing compliments. Or maybe you're married to a person who doesn't know how to make you feel special with words. Or maybe you never feel like you look marvelous—no matter how many times you hear it.

I have good news for you. God thinks you're

marvelous! He created you exactly how you are. So even if you hate your freckles or you wish you were taller, God thinks you're perfect. He adores you, and He wants you to find out just how much. Go to His Word and read how much He loves you. He tells you over and over again throughout the Bible. Spend some time with Him, and find out how marvelous God thinks you are today. (MMA)

OVERCOMING FEAR WITH LOVE

For God has not given us a spirit of fear and timidity, but of power, love, and self-discipline.

2 TIMOTHY 1:7 NLT

*M*rs. Eckles," the court clerk said, "we're ready for you."

These simple words changed Jan Eckles's life forever. Yet she had almost let fear keep her from hearing them. Most people are a bit nervous when starting a job, but Jan Eckles faced a few more obstacles than the average new employee. As an adult, a hereditary retinal disease had left her blind, and she had only recently learned to move about the city with a cane. She was also entering a brand-new field, that of court interpreter.

On that first day, an almost overwhelming sense of apprehension gripped Jan as she waited outside the courtroom. A sudden and sobering reality surged through her, making her feel inadequate with both her lack of experience as a Spanish interpreter and her limited knowledge of legal terminology. She was almost ready to back out when the court clerk came for her. Jan followed the clerk in, and with trembling hands and cramping stomach, she prepared for the frightening unknown.

That's when the promise Paul had written to Timothy rang in her ears: "For God has not given us a spirit of fear. . . ." The session began. She concentrated so intensely on each utterance that the pounding of the judge's gavel startled her. After ordering a recess, he asked Jan to approach the bench.

Painfully aware of her deficient abilities, Jan took a deep breath in preparation to receive a well-deserved reprimand. What she heard instead surprised her as much as the pounding gavel.

"Mrs. Eckles, I'm bilingual as well," the judge

said with a tender voice, "and I'm very impressed with the accuracy level of your interpretation and your professionalism."

With those words, Jan's new career took flight, and she heard in them not only the pleasure of the judge but the reassurance of God, as if He was reminding her, *"If you trust in Me, the results exceed all your expectations."* (RR)

GET OUT OF THE CAR

*"Now have come the salvation and the power
and the kingdom of our God, and the authority
of his Messiah. For the accuser of our brothers
and sisters, who accuses them before our
God day and night, has been hurled down."*

REVELATION 12:10 NIV

Have you taken any guilt trips lately?

If you answered yes, then it's time to get out of the car. Guilt is not from God. The Bible tells us that the devil—not the Lord—is the accuser of God's children. God sent Jesus to die on the cross so that we could be free.

Free is free.

The freedom that Jesus bought includes freedom from eternal damnation, freedom from fear, freedom from lack, and freedom from condemnation and guilt. You don't have to take guilt trips if you have asked Jesus to be the Lord of your life.

But the devil will still try to lure you into his car and take you on a long, depressing road trip. He loves to remind you of all the mistakes you have made. He loves to tell you that God could never love you because you have been such a bad person. He is the chauffeur of all guilt trips, ready to take you on an extended drive whenever you will let him.

Don't let him. Just get out of the car!

Maybe you're saying, "But you don't know how badly I've messed up my life. I deserve guilt. I deserve to be unhappy."

If you really feel that way, then you have fallen for the devil's lies. I want to remind you of the truth: if you have asked Jesus to forgive your sins and be Lord over your life, you are guaranteed eternal life and His joy.

The next time the devil whispers in your ear, "You don't deserve happiness because you have done too many bad things in your life," boldly answer, "I am saved. Jesus wiped away all my sins and removed them as far as the east is from the west. He no longer remembers my sins, so why should I?"

That's what the Word says—and using the Word of God against the devil is your best defense. Just say no to guilt trips. Remind the devil that you are on the road to heaven—and he can't make that trip with you. (MMA)

SHE CAN COOK TOO

But the Lord said to her, "My dear Martha, you are worried and upset over all these details! There is only one thing worth being concerned about."

LUKE 10:41-42 NLT

Call Sarah the superwoman. She can do it all. She has done every kind of nursing there is—office, hospital, psychiatric, end-of-life care, management. She's a mom, a Bible study leader, and a hostess who always comes through. She's been a deaconess as well as a church camp nurse and counselor. If all that wasn't enough, she can cook too.

Sarah makes dynamite meals for small groups—or gatherings of a hundred. In the kitchen she mixes, stirs, bakes, and orders others about with the kindness of a loving mom and the precision of a drill sergeant.

When a church wants to host a large event and feed a group of hungry people, Sarah gets called because Sarah delivers.

Most amazing of all, Sarah is content doing this sort of thing. She loves the role of hostess and cook. Whipping together special desserts for company or adapting a recipe for six to feed sixty gives Sarah a rush. She is serenely content doing what she does best in the kitchen—cooking and serving others.

But Sarah is no Martha, distracted sister of Mary. Sarah knows how to leave off the preparations and the food when there's serious work to be done. The work of prayer and spending time with God never takes a back seat to her culinary talents. Sarah is as quick and eager to "hunker down" and pray as she is to wield a spatula—even more so. Like Martha's sister, Sarah knows "there is only one thing worth being concerned about" (Luke 10:42 NLT). Sarah knows how to sit at the

feet of her Savior to listen and learn. Her stillness at His feet gives her the peace to do the tasks she loves on her own feet.

The Lord Jesus is not insensitive to those who find a measure of solace playing the role of hostess. He healed Peter's mother-in-law, who immediately went from her sickbed to waiting on those who had gathered in her home (Mark 1:30–31). The secret to serenity in doing comes with the secret of *being*.

"One thing I ask from the Lord, this only do I seek. . .to gaze on the beauty of the Lord and to seek him in his temple. For in the day of trouble he will keep me safe in his dwelling" (Psalm 27:4–5 NIV). Even when there are ten for dinner instead of six, our time at the Savior's feet is where tranquility begins. (KAD)

MAKEUP—DON'T LEAVE HOME WITHOUT IT

"The LORD does not look at the things
people look at. People look at the outward
appearance, but the LORD looks at the heart."

1 SAMUEL 16:7 NIV

My pastor leaned over the pulpit, smiled, and said, "I always tell my wife to treat her makeup like the commercial says to treat your American Express card—don't leave home without it!"

I glanced over at his wife and thought, *Yep. He is so sleeping on the pastoral couch tonight.*

All teasing aside, the dog may be man's best friend, but mascara is a lady's best bud. My mama always told me to put on a little lipstick and some mascara at the very least, because you never know who you might run into at the grocery store. She's right, of course. The one time I headed to Walmart without a speck of makeup on, I practically saw my entire high school graduating class. I wanted to hide in the display of toilet paper until all the lights were dimmed and I could bolt to my car. Ever been there?

Makeup is an amazing thing. It can hide blemishes. It can enhance your eyes. It can make thin lips look luscious and moist. It can transform stubby, faded eyelashes into long, curled, and dark lashes. It can give your cheeks color, making you appear well rested when you've been up all night.

Makeup is a gift from God—I'm sure of it!

But wouldn't it be even better if our skin had no flaws to cover? Wouldn't it be better if our lips were already the perfect shade of pink? Wouldn't it be better if our cheeks were naturally rosy and our lashes naturally thick? If we were already perfect, we wouldn't need anything to cover our imperfections.

Well, maybe our outsides aren't perfect, but

if you've asked Jesus to be your Lord and Savior, your heart is blemish-free. See, God didn't just cover our sins with His heavenly Father foundation. Instead, He sent Jesus to die for us and take away all of our sins. Isn't that good news? The moment we asked Jesus to forgive us, we became flawless on the inside. That's how God sees us—perfect and blemish-free.

The Word says that God looks on the heart, while man looks on the outward appearance. So while you might want to put a little paint on the barn before venturing out, your heart is already lovely. (MMA)

YOU CAN'T BUY
HAPPINESS

*This is how we know what love is: Jesus Christ
laid down his life for us. And we ought to lay
down our lives for our brothers and sisters.
If anyone has material possessions and sees
a brother or sister in need but has no pity
on them, how can the love of God be in that
person? Dear children, let us not love with
words or speech but with actions and in truth.*

1 JOHN 3:16–18 NIV

*A*ccording to an article in *USA Today*, you
can't buy happiness—no matter how rich
you become. In fact, University of Illinois psy-
chologist Ed Diener was quoted in the story as
saying, "Materialism is toxic for happiness."

So, contrary to popular belief, buying an entire
collection of Jimmy Choo shoes will not make one

happy. Now, I have to be honest with you: I love to shop. When I walk into a department store, my heart pounds with excitement. Sale racks full of designer clothing beckon me. Flashy handbags and sterling silver jewelry seem to dance under the store's fluorescent lighting, making a smile spread across my face. I truly enjoy shopping, so when I read this article, a part of me said, *Well, these people just don't know where to shop. I could show them happiness if they'd come to Dallas.*

But in reality, that kind of happiness is fleeting.

Do you know why? Because true happiness doesn't come from acquiring things for oneself; true happiness comes from giving to others.

I am not saying that shopping is a bad thing. I am, however, saying that Jesus' words "It is more blessed to give than to receive" (Acts 20:35 NIV) are true. God created us to be givers because we are made in His image, and He is the greatest Giver of all. He gave His one and only Son to die on a cross so that we could have eternal life with Him. As Christians, the desire to give should be strong in us too.

If you have felt unfulfilled and less than happy lately, look at your own generosity. Have you become a taker more than a giver? When is the last time you looked forward to placing a tithe in the offering plate? Have you recently done anything totally unselfish for someone else? If it has been too long, then get back into the giving mode.

Call that frazzled single mom in your neighborhood and offer to watch her children for a while. Invite that widower in your church over for dinner and fellowship. Buy school supplies for an underprivileged child. And do it all unto the Lord. You will find that giving is the greatest high—even better than discovering Jimmy Choo shoes on sale! (MMA)

PEACOCKS OF HAPPINESS

*You, L*ORD *God, have done many wonderful*
things, and you have planned marvelous
things for us. No one is like you! I would
never be able to tell all you have done.

PSALM 40:5 CEV

Hurrying into the office one afternoon, I was totally focused on an upcoming meeting. I was going over some mental notes when, all of a sudden, I looked up to see the most beautiful sight. Next to the front door of our office building stood a brilliant blue peacock grooming himself in the sun. Rays of sunlight bounced off his fabulous feathers, making the sight even more breathtaking. I literally stopped in my high heels, for a moment experiencing total joy. I wanted to squeal like a little girl on Christmas morning. I just couldn't believe my eyes!

No, I hadn't been sniffing my pink highlighter. There really was a peacock outside, which I later learned belonged to a nearby rancher. This beautiful bird liked to roam, and on this particular day, he had roamed right into my life.

As I stopped to appreciate the peacock's beauty, I thanked God for reminding me of His presence in the midst of my day—showing me love and favor even when I was caught up in the busyness of life.

The day had started like any other, but right in the middle of the mundane, God had dropped a peacock of happiness into my morning. While later contemplating my surprise visitation, I realized that God drops "peacocks of happiness" into our lives all the time. Unfortunately, we are often too busy or our hearts too hardened to notice.

You may never have a fantastic feathered friend show up outside your home or office, but be on the lookout for God's good work and lovingkindness toward you every day. Be mindful of

Him all day long, and drink in those moments of pure joy. Maybe your peacock of happiness will come in the form of your child's laughter. Or maybe your peacock will be the lovely fragrance of a honeysuckle bush. However your peacocks come, take time to enjoy them, and praise the Lord for His blessing. God loves to surprise us with good things—especially when we appreciate the "peacocks" He sends into our lives. (MMA)

WHAT A BARGAIN!

*For God so loved the world that he gave his
one and only Son, that whoever believes in
him shall not perish but have eternal life.*

JOHN 3:16 NIV

*T*here's something intoxicating about finding a
great deal. Some call it thrilling. Some call it
a shopping high. I call it pure happiness.

If you have never been to a yard sale, a con-
signment shop, or your town's Goodwill store,
you are missing out. From designer scarves to
eclectic furniture, you will find it all at these
bargain meccas. What they say about bargain
shopping is true: "One person's junk is another
person's treasure."

I have found many treasures on bargain-
hunting trips. Once I found a Louis Vuitton scarf
for only ninety-nine cents. Another time, a Carole

Little suit for three dollars. On another occasion, I came home with a Banana Republic leather jacket for only six dollars.

Those kinds of buys make you want to shout from the rooftop. But those bargains pale in comparison to the greatest bargain of all time—salvation.

God gave His only Son to die on the cross so that we could have eternal life. All we have to do is ask Him to forgive us of our sins and accept Him as our Lord and Savior. We receive eternal life, healing, peace, love, wisdom, prosperity, joy, and so much more—all free to us, since Jesus has paid the price for our sins! Now that's a bargain really worth shouting from the rooftops!

Make sure you share the love of Jesus with all those you encounter. Tell them about the treasure you have found in Jesus, and encourage them to pray this prayer with you:

Dear Father, we thank You for sending Jesus to die on the cross for us. We thank You for loving us that much. Today we ask You to forgive us of all our sins, and we accept Jesus as our Lord and Savior. We love You. Amen.

Sharing Jesus with the world around you will bring much happiness to you, and it will bring much happiness to those who accept Him as their Lord and Savior. Don't be afraid to witness for the Lord. He will open doors for you to share your faith. Just be obedient to walk through them. (MMA)

THE CONFIDENCE TO RISK EVERYTHING

*So they went and entered the house of
a prostitute named Rahab and stayed
there. . . . But the woman had taken
the two men and hidden them.*

JOSHUA 2:1, 4 NIV

*A*ny woman who thinks she needs to perfect
her life or faith before serving the Lord
should take another look at Rahab. One of the
women named in the record of faithful heroes
(see Hebrews 11:31), Rahab's early life hardly
appeared to be a model-perfect picture of morality
and belief. Her growing faith in the works of the
Lord, however, gave her the confidence to put
everything she knew at risk.

Rahab's life could not have been easy. The
text refers to her as a prostitute, although some

archaeological evidence indicates Rahab may have operated an inn, since the two jobs were often closely linked, and scripture says that the spies lodged with her. Either way, her profession was difficult and dangerous. Yet Rahab met a lot of travelers, and she had learned in great detail what was going on in her city as well as her country. Thus, while Rahab's decision to hide the Hebrew spies on her roof may seem a bit impulsive as first told in Joshua 2, she later makes it clear that this is something she'd been thinking about for some time.

When ordered by the king to surrender the spies, she quickly hid the men on the roof and covered them with flax. She then explained to the king's messenger that the spies had already departed, risking a charge of treason. After the king's men left, however, Rahab confronted the two Israelites about what the Lord had been doing and asked for their help (see Joshua 2:8–13).

She had been listening to her clients and

marveling at all the Lord had done in Canaan. Although other citizens of Jericho probably knew as much as she did about the conquests of Israel, this quick-thinking and intelligent woman was the only one to put more faith in God than in the fortifications of her city. Believing instead that Jericho would never stand against the power of God, Rahab chose to follow the Lord, no matter what the cost.

Her faith saved her family—and this strong woman became one of the ancestors of Jesus Christ. Her example reminds us today that no matter what our background or circumstances, what God wants most of all is simply our trust and love. (RR)

REFUGE

"May you be richly rewarded by the
LORD, the God of Israel, under whose
wings you have come to take refuge."

RUTH 2:12 NIV

*I*n the days when the judges ruled, there was a
famine in the land" (Ruth 1:1 NIV). That's how
the book bearing Ruth's name begins. It follows
immediately on the heels of a book that ends with
similarly bleak words: "In those days Israel had
no king; everyone did as they saw fit" (Judges
21:25 NIV). From this setting a Jewish man and
his wife, Naomi, move to Moab. Ultimately their
two sons marry women of this country. And so
begins the story of Ruth, the great-grandmother
of Israel's greatest king, David.

When Ruth, like her mother-in-law and sister-
in-law, is widowed, she decides to go to Israel with

Naomi, her Jewish mother-in-law. There's nothing to suggest that Ruth had ever visited or lived in Israel, but she chooses to remain by Naomi's side and return there with her. Something in the very first chapter of the book hints at Ruth's source of serenity in a time often unkind to women—and in a culture unfriendly toward Moabites, which is what Ruth was.

"Where you go I will go," she tells her mother-in-law. "Your people will be my people and your God my God. Where you die I will die, and there I will be buried. May the LORD deal with me. . .if even death separates you and me" (Ruth 1:16–17 NIV). Ruth's sureness of this move to unfamiliar country is not anchored in Naomi but in the God she has come to call by His holy name—the Lord. She chooses to leave the familiar but pagan nature gods of her homeland to live with those who, like her, worship the one true God, the Lord God of Israel.

The love story between Ruth and an older man

named Boaz dominates the rest of Ruth's story. Although Naomi encourages Ruth to work in the fields of Boaz for her own safety, Boaz himself tells Ruth that the God of Israel is the One under whose wings she has come to take refuge (Ruth 2:12). Ruth's future husband recognized that this young woman's security was not linked to his protection. It was linked to the Lord their God.

If we're facing a move to another city or country, our source of safety can be the same as Ruth's. Not allowing the familiarity of the past or the uncertainty of the future to dictate our inner state allows God to work His peace in us. He "will keep in perfect peace all who trust in [Him]" (Isaiah 26:3 NLT). (KAD)

GOD IS AT WORK

I am trusting you, O LORD, saying, "You are my God!" My future is in your hands.

PSALM 31:14-15 NLT

*D*id you know that God is often working most when we sense it the least?

As I reflect on my life, I can see that has often been the case. Those times when things looked the worst, when it seemed as if God had gone on vacation, were the times when God was working behind the scenes on my behalf.

We discover that our timing is not always God's timing. Actually, our timing is almost never God's timing. We want instant gratification in our give-it-to-me-now society. We want to pray and have God answer us by noon. But God usually doesn't work like that.

Take it from Noah.

He followed God's leading and built an ark—even though it had never rained before. He obeyed God's instructions perfectly. Pairs of all the animals began to fill the big boat, and finally, Noah and his family boarded the ark and waited for the rain.

You know the story. It rained forty days and forty nights, and Noah and his family were the only ones spared. The boat ride, however, was much longer than forty days. It went on for months and months! Think about that for a moment: Noah and his family are on an ark with a bunch of smelly animals for months on end, and there's no land in sight. Can't you just hear his wife saying, "Yeah, great plan, Noah. Where's the land? Did God tell you how long we'd have to float around with a bunch of stinking creatures?"

You can imagine Noah, every day looking out the ark's windows, only to see water on every side. Finally, Noah sends out a bird, hoping to get proof that land has appeared somewhere—but the bird comes back empty beaked. It must have looked like God had forgotten them, that they were doomed to ride around on a big boat forever.

But God was at work, slowly diminishing the water every day—even those days when Noah saw water all around. In time the ark hit dry land, and Noah and his family left the ark to enjoy God's promise.

Are you on a long ark ride right now? If so, rejoice! Be happy today—even if you can't see anything changing. Land is near. God hasn't forgotten you. He is at work behind the scenes. (MMA)

WHERE ARE YOU LOOKING?

"For my thoughts are not your thoughts, neither are your ways my ways," declares the LORD. "As the heavens are higher than the earth, so are my ways higher than your ways and my thoughts than your thoughts."

ISAIAH 55:8-9 NIV

Helen Keller used to say, "When one door of happiness closes, another opens; but often we look so long at the closed door that we do not see the one which has opened for us."

Most everyone has read the story of Helen Keller. She was born a healthy, happy child in Tuscumbia, Alabama, on June 27, 1880. But at the age of nineteen months, she suddenly lost her hearing and vision as a result of illness—possibly scarlet fever. Her life was forever changed. She was forced to grow up in a hearing and seeing world she didn't understand, one that didn't always embrace her.

Her story is one of great persistence and triumph over adversity. Beating overwhelming odds, this highly intelligent, sensitive woman devoted her life to bettering those around her.

You might say she chose to look for the open doors.

Let me ask you this: Are you looking for the open doors in your life? When one door closes, do you stand there staring at it, longing to batter it down? Or do you trust God for another door of happiness?

The Word tells us that God's ways are higher than our ways and His thoughts are higher than our thoughts (Isaiah 55:9). In other words, He may close a door that you're sure is the only one that will ever lead to happiness. You may plead with Him, "Please! Open the door!" And all the while, He is trying to get your eyes back on Him so He can show you the even better door of happiness that He has waiting for you.

So don't waste any more time staring at the closed doors in your life. Get your eyes back on God and let Him show you that next door of happiness. It may be right in front of you. (MMA)

SWEET FRAGRANCES

*The LORD smelled the pleasing aroma
and said in his heart: "Never again will
I curse the ground because of humans."*

GENESIS 8:21 NIV

ragrance is a powerful thing. Colognes, candles, flowers, and room fresheners attest to the popularity of sweet smells. If you want to sell your house, Realtors tell you to bake bread or boil orange peels and cinnamon on the stove before showings.

Some women (and men, I suspect) hunt for a cologne that becomes their signature fragrance. Simmering potpourri invites us to take a deep breath. One whiff of a significant aroma can instantly transport us to a different time and place. A fresh bouquet of roses can bring a delighted "Mmmmm" to our lips—or a tickle and a sneeze

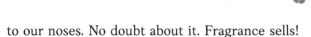

to our noses. No doubt about it. Fragrance sells!

One of the first mentions of fragrance in the Bible follows the world's most devastating disaster of all time: the flood of Noah's day. Man's sin had become a stench in the nostrils of God Almighty. He decided to end the rampant sin. Only Noah and his family escaped God's wrath. When the rain finally ceased and Noah and his family stepped on solid ground for the first time in months, Noah's first act was one of worship.

"So Noah came out, together with his sons and his wife and his sons' wives. . . . Then Noah built an altar to the LORD and. . .sacrificed burnt offerings on it" (Genesis 8:18, 20 NIV). From the sweet fragrance that found its way to the heavens came God's promise to maintain earth's cycle of seasons as long as the earth remains (v. 22).

Since we are made in God's image, fragrance can work powerfully in us too. Lighting an aromatic candle may quiet us after a full day. Sinking into a bathtub filled with fragrant bubble bath may relax our tense muscles. Inhaling the satisfying smell of hazelnut coffee before taking a sip may soften our furrowed brow.

Sweet contentment through our olfactory sense—such simple delight!

Today you may be having the greatest time of your life. Your best friend may be having her worst. Since God calls us "the pleasing aroma of Christ" and "an aroma that brings life" (2 Corinthians 2:15–16 NIV), you may want to take your aromatic self to the side of your disconsolate friend. Maybe you can bring an hour of contentment to her just by being there. While you're at it, you may want to take along something that smells good. A sense of contentment may be as close as a pleasant whiff of flowers or a steaming cup of herbal tea. (KAD)

BRING ON THE
LEG WARMERS

*Jesus Christ is the same yesterday
and today and forever.*

HEBREWS 13:8 NIV

*A*hhh. . .the eighties. I remember them well. I graduated from Bedford, Indiana's North Lawrence High School in 1987, so I am an eighties lady. Oh yeah. I had hair so big I could hardly fit into my red Fiero. I practically had to use a can of hair spray a day to keep those big ol' bangs sky-high. I wore the neon-colored plastic bracelets up my arms—just like Madonna. And I even had a pair of leg warmers. Scary, huh?

Yeah, my daughters think my senior yearbook is pretty hilarious.

Even if you're not an eighties lady, I bet there were some fashion fiascoes from your time too. For example, what was with that caked-on, baby-blue eye shadow of the seventies? Yuck! Fashion trends come and go. One week, the fashion magazines say, "Long jackets are hip. The longer the better. . ." And the next week, the fashion trend reads, "Cropped, military-style jackets are the rage! Long coats are short on fashion savvy. . . ." Ugh! Let's face it. It's almost impossible to keep up with the times.

Fads come and go. Styles change. And the way clothes fit our bodies definitely changes over time. (Can I hear an "Amen"?) Change is inevitable. From changing fashions to changing locations to changing diapers—as women, we're in the "changing" mode most of our lives. So in the midst of all this change, isn't it good to know that God never changes? Malachi 3:6 says, "I the LORD do not change" (NIV).

You can always count on the Lord. He's there through thick and thin, leg warmers and parachute pants and everything in between. Let Him be the stability in your life. Run to God when you feel overwhelmed by the changes going on around you. If you'll stay grounded in Him, you'll always be "heavenly hip" and ready to face anything—even if spandex stirrup pants make a comeback! (MMA)

TREASURED

*But his mother treasured all
these things in her heart.*

LUKE 2:51 NIV

*T*his is how the birth of Jesus the Messiah came about: His mother Mary was pledged to be married to Joseph, but before they came together, she was found to be pregnant through the Holy Spirit" (Matthew 1:18 NIV). So begins our introduction to Mary, the mother of God incarnate, the Lord Jesus Christ.

After her obvious question to the angel who brought the news that she would birth the Messiah into the world, we read Mary's unabashed statements: "I am the Lord's servant. . . . May your word to me be fulfilled" (Luke 1:38 NIV). *That,* dear woman of God, is serenity!

We are given only snapshots of Mary scattered

throughout the New Testament. Whenever we encounter this unique woman, an air of peace drapes itself around the scene. When she shares the news of her miraculous pregnancy and the product of that pregnancy (the Savior of the world), she sings. In her song she quotes passages from the Old Testament books of Habakkuk, the Psalms, Exodus, and Genesis (see Luke 1:46–55). When shepherds heard about the Messiah's birth and saw the infant Christ for themselves, they noised it about. Mary, however, "treasured up all these things and pondered them in her heart" (Luke 2:19 NIV).

Decades later, Mary saves a new groom embarrassment by referring the servants to her Son for the provision of more wine at a wedding reception (see John 2:1–10). At Jesus' death, and then again after His resurrection, she is a breath of shadowy calm at the horror of Christ's crucifixion and at the birth of the Christian church (see John 19:25–26; Acts 1:14).

What was Mary's secret? Like the woman herself, the answer is tucked away in some unpretentious verses. She was "highly favored" of the Lord, who was with her (Luke 1:28 NIV). When we read her glorious song of praise to God later in the chapter, all her focus is centered in this One who is with her. "My soul glorifies the Lord," she says, "and my spirit rejoices in God my Savior. . . . the Mighty One has done great things for me. . . . His mercy extends to those who fear him. . . . He has performed mighty deeds with his arm" (Luke 1:46–47, 49–51 NIV). As a young girl visited by an angel or as a grown woman who watched her Son die and return to life again, Mary never let go of the marvelous truth that brought her comfort: God has a mind full of those He loves (see Luke 1:48 and Psalm 8:4). (KAD)

FIND YOUR PRECEDENT

When Elkanah slept with Hannah, the LORD
remembered her plea, and in due time she
gave birth to a son. She named him Samuel,
for she said, "I asked the LORD for him."

1 SAMUEL 1:19-20 NLT

The Bible is more than just a good book filled with great stories. It's alive. It's pertinent. It's full of promises. It's our lifeline! So why do so many of us leave it on the coffee table instead of discovering its power and relevance today?

My oldest niece, Mandy, found out just how powerful and alive the Word of God is when she began believing for a baby. She and her husband, Chris, tried for several years to conceive, but every month the pregnancy test came back negative. She was discouraged. Lots of people gave her advice: "Take this vitamin, and it will help you get pregnant"; "Try conceiving when there is a full moon";

"Stop eating acidic food, and you'll have a greater chance of success." Mandy followed every bit of advice, trying desperately to become pregnant—but the only thing she became was depressed.

Then her mother suggested, "Mandy, honey, why don't you find some scriptures to stand on? Find your promises in the Word of God and pray them over yourself every single day. The Word works!"

Mandy had been a Christian since she was a little girl, so she was certainly open to the suggestion. Since that was about the only thing she hadn't tried, Mandy was willing to give the Word a shot. She dug into the Bible and found the story of how Sarah had given birth to Isaac. Then she found the story of how Hannah had believed God for a baby and finally had given birth to Samuel and several other children, too.

Mandy found a precedent in the Word of God and asked God to do for her what He had done for Sarah and Hannah. And He did! She stood on those scriptures for three months, and that's when her pregnancy test came back positive. Mandy gave birth to a healthy baby boy on February 15, 2006.

Jesus once told a story of an oppressed widow who pestered a judge until she got the justice she so desperately wanted. The moral of the story? According to Jesus, people "should always pray and not give up" (Luke 18:1 NIV).

Not every prayer will be answered the way we may hope. Even Jesus asked His Father if the trauma of the crucifixion could be avoided—but concluded His prayer with the words "yet not my will, but yours be done" (Luke 22:42 NIV).

God has promises for all of us—promises of an abundant life and of peace, hope, and joy. Those universal promises may also include personal blessings for our families, workplaces, and churches. So dust off that Bible and find what God says about your situation. The Word works all the time. Now that's something to be happy about! (MMA)

HARMONY, MELODY, AND RHYTHM

Be filled with the Spirit; speaking to
yourselves in psalms and hymns and
spiritual songs, singing and making
melody in your heart to the Lord.

EPHESIANS 5:18-19 KJV

While growing up and as a grown woman, I've always appreciated my mother's humming. When she's working in the kitchen, cleaning, or doing a project, she's humming. The only time it ceased for a long season was in the first months or year after my dad died. But as He does, God wrought His healing in my mom's brokenness, and she's back to her humming self. One of the nurses I work with is a hummer too. I find it pleasant and even infectious. One night at work I was mindlessly doing it too, hardly conscious

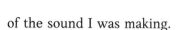

of the sound I was making.

"Excuse me," said one of my coworkers. I looked up to face a scowl. "Would you mind? That noise is very irritating."

So much for all of us enjoying someone else's humming. It must be why God had Paul write, make "melody *in your heart* to the Lord" (emphasis added). Not everyone enjoys listening to another's melodic musings.

Music in all its forms is a powerful motivator, isn't it? There's hardly a movie made that doesn't have music playing in the background. Hitler was quick to use music to rouse his armies to a passionate fervor for "the fatherland." We use lullabies to quiet infants and praise songs to inspire worship and focus on God. Even computer games and pinball machines have a "music" of sorts to engage the user.

Have you ever thought about how the Lord Jesus sounded when He sang? Before He and the disciples went out to the Mount of Olives, they sang a hymn (Mark 14:26). Did the Lord have a rich, low baritone or a soaring tenor voice? God has built music into creation because His is the first voice. Not only do the stars sing (Job 38:7), but God sings too. "The LORD your God is with you," Zephaniah says, and "[He] will rejoice over you with singing" (Zephaniah 3:17 NIV). In an unhurried moment, "with his love, he will calm all your fears" (Zephaniah 3:17 NLT).

In sign language the gesture for singing or music is a fluid motion of one hand over another. That "says" music can be soothing. Is your day today hectic or out of control? It may be time to put on some music, put those fingers on the piano keys, or hum your favorite praise song. Let a little music breathe a measure of serenity into your hurried day. (KAD)

GOD GIVES YOU WISDOM

If any of you need wisdom, you should ask
God, and it will be given to you. God is
generous and won't correct you for asking.

JAMES 1:5 CEV

The older I've gotten, the more I've heard myself uttering the words, "Well, as my mother used to say. . ." It's almost become a joke among my friends, and they'll start to grin even before I can get some pithy proverb out. In fact, some of my mother's sayings are quite humorous, filled with homespun advice and earthy metaphors, like the day she was canning some beans and told me she was "hotter than a tent preacher in July." We're from Alabama, and I can assure you that camp meetings in the summer can get pretty hot!

It's not just the down-to-earth proverbs, however, that I depend on. My mother's wisdom sometimes amazes me. I began to ask her advice on people and situations when I was still just a kid, and she has seldom steered me wrong. When a kid was trying to bully me in junior high school, her advice helped me ease the situation in just a few days. When dealing with a variety of men in college had me spinning in confusion, she helped me find my feet again. She taught me how to handle money, work, and even my faith.

I once asked her about the source of her wisdom, and she responded, "A little bit of living and a whole lot of prayer."

My mother had learned to rely on God for guidance and inspiration, which had made her invaluable to her friends and family. Even the tiniest problems were turned over to God, which gave her the confidence to help out those who came to her for advice.

I think it's very revealing that wisdom in scripture is portrayed as a woman (see Proverbs 1:20–21), since women seem to have an

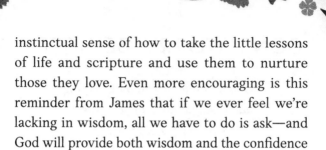

instinctual sense of how to take the little lessons of life and scripture and use them to nurture those they love. Even more encouraging is this reminder from James that if we ever feel we're lacking in wisdom, all we have to do is ask—and God will provide both wisdom and the confidence to use it. (RR)

DON'T WORRY, BE HAPPY

*"Can any one of you by worrying
add a single hour to your life?"*

MATTHEW 6:27 NIV

Remember that eighties song "Don't Worry, Be Happy"? (You're singing along right now, aren't you?) Well, it's not only a fun song with a great reggae beat, but it's also good advice. "Don't worry, be happy" is a good motto to adopt, because worry will steal your joy faster than you can say "leg warmers."

Worry is a sneaky thing. You might start the day just thinking about a situation in your life, but if you think too long, you will end up in full-out worry mode. You will start thinking things like, *If those layoffs really happen at our company, I don't know what we'll do. We just barely make it now. What if I can't get another job with*

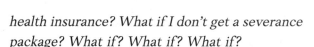

health insurance? What if I don't get a severance package? What if? What if? What if?

Don't let your thoughts take you there. If you cross over into the land of worry, you will eventually drive into the territory of fear and ultimately hit the city limits of despair. It's not worth it! Besides, no matter how much you worry, it doesn't change the situation one single bit, right? Prayer is what changes things.

Worry is not only a happiness stealer but a sin. The Bible instructs us not to worry. Matthew 6:34 says, "Therefore do not worry about tomorrow, for tomorrow will worry about itself. Each day has enough trouble of its own" (NIV).

That's pretty clear, isn't it?

Worry is a hard habit to break, especially if you have lived your whole life as a worrywart. But it's not impossible to overcome. How do I know? I was a world-class worrier for many years. I'd think about something for a while and eventually work myself into such a tizzy that I wanted to hide under the covers and eat bonbons all day. Ever been there?

If you have been taking regular trips to the land of worry, get off that highway. Take the prayer detour and stay on that road until you reach your final destination of peace, happiness, and victory. And while you're "in the car," pop in an eighties CD and sing along with "Don't Worry, Be Happy." Good tunes always make the journey more fun! (MMA)

WITH SPIT, DIRT, AND A HAIRPIN

I lie awake; I have become
like a bird alone on a roof.

PSALM 102:7 NIV

Locked in separate cells, the missionary doctor and her physician husband found themselves in a Manchurian concentration camp. Days without change in routine or surroundings loomed before Dr. Byram. She didn't know how long she would be in her solitary cell. She didn't know if she'd emerge from it alive. All she had with her was her Bible.

Where can a woman find serenity while imprisoned in a foreign land without friend, family, or aid of any kind close at hand? Being used to busy days and nights of ministry and healing, how would she now pass these interminable hours alone? Could she find any meaning in this? Could she keep her sanity?

Dr. Byram opened her Bible and began reading. She decided to study the Word of God from cover to cover. She had no paper, no pen, no means readily at hand to record all her thoughts and insights to keep, should she ever get out of solitary confinement. She scratched her head, and her finger touched something hard and straight.

She withdrew the hairpin from her hair and studied it for a moment. She stuck the end of it in her mouth and then put the tip in the dust of her dirt floor. She pressed it to a page of her Bible. It worked!

Until she was released from prison, this woman penned the thoughts and reflections of her solitary Bible study with a hairpin, her saliva, and the dirt of her cell floor. She never forgot her time alone with God in that solitary cell. Meticulously recorded in her Bible, her solitary lessons were carefully inscribed on her soul as well.

From that experience in Manchuria, Dr. Byram became a woman of prayer like few others. Once free from her imprisonment, she spent ninety minutes of every day for the rest of her life in prayer. She learned the key to serenity (and prayer) in solitary confinement.

Sometimes we may feel as if we're in solitary confinement. Our health keeps us homebound, or friends and family have died or moved away. We may have more time alone—like a lone bird on a roof—than we wish. Can we do with those hours, days, weeks, and months what this missionary doctor did with hers?

Jesus has never made a promise He can't or won't keep. "Be sure of this: I am with you always, even to the end of the age" (Matthew 28:20 NLT). (KAD)

IS YOUR GLASS HALF-FULL?

*Rejoice always, pray continually, give
thanks in all circumstances; for this is
God's will for you in Christ Jesus.*

1 THESSALONIANS 5:16-18 NIV

*A*re you a glass-half-empty or a glass-half-
full person?

You might say that's a foolish question because,
either way, it's just half a glass. Quantitatively, that's
true. What you think doesn't increase or decrease
the actual amount of liquid in the glass. But *qual-
itatively* it makes a huge difference—between an
unhappy or a happy existence.

A few years ago, the media company I worked
for experienced a difficult financial year. As the
holidays approached, we received a memo that
read,

Due to our challenging financial year, we are unable to give you, our treasured employees, Christmas bonuses this holiday season.

The letter continued with a heartfelt apology, a plea for patience, and a prayer for a better year.

When the infamous memo arrived on our desks, the glass-half-empty people were livid! To be honest, we glass-half-full folks weren't exactly doing the dance of Christmas joy either—but the difference between the two groups' reactions was vast.

The glass-half-empty employees griped for months. If they were asked to do anything beyond the norm, they would grudgingly comply—then say something sarcastic like, "Yeah, we'd be happy to get right on that because our company has done so much for us lately." The glass-half-full folks, on the other hand, continued to work hard and hope for a better future.

The following December, we received another envelope on our desks, but this time it didn't contain just a memo. It held a memo and a Christmas bonus check. Sighs of relief and whoops of celebration rang out in the glass-half-full camp. Guess what the glass-half-empty group did?

They complained.

"Well, it's about time!" was heard from certain cubicles. Or "Better late than never!" or "Too little too late, if you ask me."

It was a good lesson—one I'll never forget. I saw firsthand how glass-half-empty folks and glass-half-full people handle life's day-to-day ups and downs. The bottom line? I discovered that glass-half-full people live happier, fuller lives than the glass-half-empty folks. When faced with exactly the same circumstances, one group chose to be happy and the other depressed.

So I ask you again: Are you a glass-half-empty person or a glass-half-full person? If your glass looks half-empty today, fill up on God and change your perspective. The level in your glass may not change, but your level of happiness will! (MMA)

CONFIDENCE TO PASS ON YOUR FAITH

I am reminded of your sincere faith,
which first lived in your grandmother
Lois and in your mother Eunice and,
I am persuaded, now lives in you also.

2 TIMOTHY 1:5 NIV

*I*t's a truism we hear repeated all the time: Parents are the single greatest influence on their children. Children watch and listen, especially when they're young, absorbing the way their parents act as well as listening to what they say. This is one reason that Lois and Eunice have been recognized for passing on their "genuine faith," taking care to teach Timothy the holy scriptures, an important step in leading him to be "wise for salvation through faith" (2 Timothy 3:15 NIV).

Lois and Eunice were Jews, who had most

likely been converted by Paul when he stopped in Lystra during his first missionary journey. Already grounded with a firm faith in the Lord, they accepted Christ and continued to grow and practice their new faith with an unwavering confidence. Timothy, because of the sound background his mother and grandmother had given him, also accepted the call to Jesus, becoming a second-generation leader in the new church.

Handing down our faith across the generations is a vital gift we can give our children, and the bonds across the years don't have to be blood alone. Many of the wisest people in our lives may be our spiritual kin and unrelated by genetics. Each generation has great gifts to share in wisdom, life experiences, and a deeper understanding of scripture that sometimes comes just through walking with Christ for decades.

Mothers to daughters, grandmothers to grand-daughters, mentors to the younger people in their spiritual care. We all can look at the beautiful

lessons that Lois and Eunice passed on, and we can see the need and have the confidence to reach out to our own. Although we have no idea what kind of adults they will become, the teachings of the Lord will remain with them forever. (RR)

YOU'RE QUALIFIED

But Moses said to God, "Who am I that I should go to Pharaoh and bring the Israelites out of Egypt?"

EXODUS 3:11 NIV

I recently read a bumper sticker that said, GOD DOESN'T CALL THE QUALIFIED; HE QUALIFIES THE CALLED.

That's good, isn't it?

In a world that demands qualifications for just about everything, isn't it nice that God demands only our willingness to serve Him? In fact, God calls imperfect people.

Look at Moses. God had a huge job for him in spite of the fact that Moses had killed an Egyptian, hid him in the sand, and then fled Egypt because he was afraid of what would happen to him.

Not exactly a glowing résumé, is it?

Besides that, Moses had a speech problem—

yet God was asking him to approach Pharaoh and tell him to let God's people go free. Moses knew he wasn't qualified. In fact, he said to God, "Pardon your servant, Lord, I have never been eloquent, neither in the past nor since you have spoken to your servant. I am slow of speech and tongue" (Exodus 4:10 NIV).

But the Lord already knew that, and He still wanted Moses for the job. He said to Moses, "Who gave human beings their mouths? Who makes them deaf or mute? Who gives them sight or makes them blind? Is it not I, the LORD? Now go; I will help you speak and will teach you what to say" (Exodus 4:11–12 NIV). God already knew that Moses wasn't a gifted orator. He already knew all of Moses' shortcomings, but He still chose Moses to lead the people of Israel out of Egypt into the Promised Land.

Guess what? God knows all of your shortcomings too—and He doesn't care. He wants to use you anyway. God doesn't need your qualifications or abilities. He just wants your willing heart and availability. He will take care of the rest.

So trust Him today and be encouraged. You are qualified in God's eyes. You can be excited and happy about your life because God has a plan, and it's a good one (see Jeremiah 29:11). You may not feel qualified to do the things God has called you to do, but God is more than qualified—and He's got your back! (MMA)

GOD CHOOSES YOU

As you come to him, the living Stone—
rejected by humans but chosen by God and
precious to him—you also, like living stones,
are being built into a spiritual house to be a
holy priesthood, offering spiritual sacrifices
acceptable to God through Jesus Christ.

1 PETER 2:4-5 NIV

orn only two years before the first women's rights convention in 1850, Mary Slessor gave a whole new meaning to the idea of freedom for women.

Redheaded and bright-eyed, Mary knew even as a child that she wanted to be a missionary. She felt God had chosen her to follow in David Livingstone's footsteps, even though she had some growing up to do first. When her family moved to Dundee in 1859, she took a job in a jute mill, working half a day, then going to school the other half. By the age of fourteen, she was a skilled weaver who diligently continued her studies.

At twenty-eight, she finally realized her dream and was assigned to Calabar by the Foreign Mission Board. There she created quite a stir by going against all the norms for women missionaries. Abandoning her corsets and veils, she dressed in the style of the tribes she worked with and learned to speak Efik, so that she could use humor and sarcasm in her confrontations with some tribal customs.

And confront she did! She had a great respect for the people among whom she lived, and they understood that. This respect gave her freedom to attack such practices as ritual killing of twins, who were thought to be conceived by devils. Mary convinced the tribal leaders that twins were a sign of male virility instead. She also worked for more dignity for women and battled the enslavement of girls and wives. One anecdote told of Mary Slessor was that she once came upon a group

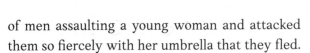

of men assaulting a young woman and attacked them so fiercely with her umbrella that they fled.

Mary's confidence to do God's will knew no bounds, and the local tribes in West Africa embraced her, calling her the "mother of all peoples." She continued to work deeper into the heart of the country, loving the people and bringing them messages of hope and freedom as well as the Word of God. She lived longer than many of her missionary colleagues, which some thought was due to her sheer will to survive.

She succumbed to a fever in January 1915 at the age of sixty-six.

Mary Slessor, with her love of God and her determination to help people, stands as a model to prove exactly how much can be done when we have confidence in the God-chosen path for our lives. (RR)

NO MORE BUG JUICE

But the Holy Spirit produces this kind
of fruit in our lives: love, joy, peace,
patience, kindness, goodness, faithfulness,
gentleness, and self-control.

GALATIANS 5:22-23 NLT

All of the gals in our Bible study have a secret saying we use to keep each other in line. When one of us starts acting ugly, a loving sister in Christ will whisper, "Bug juice." The meaning behind it? Well, when you squash a bug, what comes out? Bug juice! And believe me, it ain't pretty!

In other words, when we're under pressure, whatever is on the inside of us is what will come out. If it's bug juice, that's what spews out. If it's love, joy, peace, patience, kindness, goodness, faithfulness, gentleness, and self-control—that's what comes out. That's why we need to spend much time in the Word of God, filling ourselves with more of Jesus and His promises. Not long ago, my friend Susan was able to put this "bug juice" principle to the test when her daughter, Schalen, was in a very serious automobile accident. When Schalen was admitted into intensive care with a broken neck and blood clots on the brain, panic filled the waiting room. The situation looked very bleak. As the doctors shared the severity of Schalen's injuries with the family, Susan stood strong. Through tears, she declared, "I will not fear. God is in control. Schalen is healed in Jesus' name!"

When the pressure of the situation pressed heavily upon Susan, no bug juice oozed out. The only thing coming out of Susan was faith-filled words. She quoted scriptures and praised God for Schalen's whole and strong body.

Susan's positive attitude and faith-filled statements changed the entire atmosphere of that waiting room. In less than twenty-four hours,

Schalen rounded the corner. In forty-eight hours, they had her up and walking. Only a week later, Schalen walked across the stage at Bedford North Lawrence High School to accept her diploma.

Maybe you are in a high-pressure situation right now, and bug juice is about to blow! Ask God to develop the fruit of the Spirit on the inside of you. Spend some time today in God's Word. Meditate on His promises, and rest in Him. Pretty soon, bug juice will be a thing of the past, and only beautiful love and faith will flow out of you. You'll emanate Jesus' love when the pressure is on. And like Susan, you'll change the atmosphere around you. There's already enough bug juice out there. Why not fill your world with beauty today? (MMA)

THE CONFIDENCE TO HAVE UNWAVERING FAITH

She said to herself, "If I only touch his
cloak, I will be healed." Jesus turned and
saw her. "Take heart, daughter," he said,
"your faith has healed you." And the
woman was healed at that moment.

MATTHEW 9:21-22 NIV

Twelve years. For twelve long years, this woman had bled, in more ways than just physically. Her illness rendered her "unclean" by Jewish standards, and her family and friends would have most likely ostracized her. If she was married, her husband wouldn't have been allowed to touch her. The doctors she had sought out had taken her savings, leaving her needy, hopeless, and desperate (see Luke 8:43).

Then she heard about Jesus. She heard about

the healings He had performed, knew that He spoke the word of God. Finally, there was hope. If only she could get to Him! Taking a chance, she pushed through the crowd, firmly believing that if she could touch the mere hem of His garment, she could be healed.

Luke also wrote of this moment, saying that Jesus immediately knew that power had gone out of Him, and He turned, saying, "Who touched me?" (Luke 8:45 NIV). The disciples were astonished. With all the people pushing and shoving at Him, how could He possibly distinguish one touch from another?

He knew, however, as did the woman, who was now terrified. She was unclean, and she had dared to touch a rabbi. She fell to her knees before Him, trembling, as she explained why she had reached out to Him.

Jesus' response, however, was one of compassion and assurance. He was impressed with the simple clarity of her faith, and He comforted her and declared her healed.

Although Jewish society at the time did not always value women, Jesus did. He reached out to them, befriended and healed them, and honored them in His ministry. Nothing has changed; Jesus still cherishes each one of us.

Although trials and illness are a part of being human, our faith can remain strong in light of His love. (RR)

BE JOYFUL,
NO MATTER WHAT!

Rejoice in the Lord always.
I will say it again: Rejoice!
PHILIPPIANS 4:4 NIV

In Paul's letter to the church at Philippi, he mentions *joy* or *rejoicing* more than a dozen times. What makes that so amazing is this: Paul was in prison when he wrote Philippians. And it wasn't just any old jail. Greek scholar Rick Renner studied the historic details of the prison where Paul was held and recently shared those findings with our church. It seems that this Roman prison was known as one of the worst in the entire empire.

The prison had actually been used as a septic pit for many years, and over time had evolved into a lockup for the worst offenders. Prisoners were chained with their arms above their heads and forced to stand in human waste up to their hips. The prisoners had to stand at all times—no matter how weary they became. Since the prison had no windows or ventilation, the smell must have been horrid. In fact, many prisoners died from toxic fumes. Others died from rat bites and infection. Still others died from hopelessness.

The prison was *that* bad—so awful it sucked life itself out of many strong men.

So how could the great apostle write about rejoicing in the Lord? Paul had learned that the source of his joy had nothing to do with his environment or his physical state. He found his joy in Jesus Christ. It was God's own Son who enabled Paul to write: "Rejoice in the Lord always. I will say it again: Rejoice!"

Paul was surrounded by darkness, dung, and doom—but his heart was full of Jesus and joy. He fixed his eyes on eternal things. Paul knew that the Lord was with him in his suffering, and he knew that Jesus would deliver him from that place of despair.

So how is your joy level today? Take a lesson from the apostle Paul—rejoice no matter what! God is with you. He loves you, and He's completely aware of your situation. Don't be moved by your circumstances—even if you are waist deep in debt, sickness, marital problems, physical addictions, or whatever. God is able to deliver you. So rejoice in the Lord always—again I say, rejoice! (MMA)

LEARNING TO LISTEN

"Be still, and know that I am God."

PSALM 46:10 NIV

et's face it. We like to talk. The *Farmers' Almanac* reports that the average woman speaks twenty-five thousand more words per day than the average man. No wonder the men in our lives "tune us out" from time to time. Listening is almost a lost art form today. The late Brenda Ueland, a prolific Minnesota author and columnist, once wrote: "We should all know this: that listening, not talking, is the gifted and great role, and the imaginative role. And the true listener is much more beloved and magnetic than the talker, and she is more effective and learns more and does more good."

My friend Darlene recently learned how attractive good listening skills can be. She sat next to a woman at her son's ball game, and since she'd never met the woman before, Darlene asked her several questions. The woman answered her inquiries all night long—never once asking Darlene to share any information in return.

Later that week, the gabby woman's daughter told Darlene how much her mother had enjoyed their conversation at the ball game. Darlene had to smile at the daughter's comment. It had been a one-sided conversation, but apparently it was just what the woman had needed, and Darlene was glad to have obliged.

Many times, we're so eager to share our witty comments or tell a funny story to make ourselves seem more attractive that we don't actually listen to the speaker. No, we're too busy "rehearsing" our responses in our minds, waiting for the first opportunity to interrupt and dazzle those around us.

Are you guilty of interrupting? Do you lack listening skills? If you're like most women, you do.

And that's not a very attractive trait. No matter how pretty you might be on the outside, if you're constantly interrupting and talking over others, people will not see you in a good light.

People love a good listener—especially the men in our lives. If you'll hang on his every word, he'll talk to you more often. Practice listening today. You just might learn that talking is way overrated. (MMA)

AS A LITTLE CHILD

The wolf will live with the lamb, the
leopard will lie down with the goat, the
calf and the lion and the yearling together;
and a little child will lead them.

ISAIAH 11:6 NIV

*T*oddler Gabrielle does have a favorite holiday, but it's not Halloween. When scary goblins, ghosts, and monsters start making their appearance at the end of October, the usually gregarious Gabrielle hides behind her mother's legs. That gives her a moment of perceived safety, but that isn't where she finds her peace. Her mother overheard this spontaneous burst of prayer as soon as they got into the car. "Dear Jesus, you know I scared of those monsters. They are bad. I no like them. Please keep me safe, Jesus. Don't let them hurt me. I know you keep me safe, Jesus. I know you do." Without an amen, but with the confident faith of a child, Gabrielle made the instantaneous transition back to her usual talkative, happy self.

Think back to when you were a little girl. Did you worry about getting to Grandma's when it was snowing? Hardly. The truth was plain and simple: *We're going to Grandma's!* And, better than best, it was snowing too! Did you stew for hours over what to wear to a party? No. You were thrilled to be invited! Did you worry about dog hair in the house? Hardly—you were tickled that you got to have a puppy all your own!

It didn't take much back then to keep us content. When Jesus wants us to consider contentment, He tells us to check out growing things— lilies and children, to name two. "And why do you worry about clothes? See how the flowers of the field grow. They do not labor or spin. Yet. . .not even Solomon in all his splendor was dressed like one of these" (Matthew 6:28–29 NIV).

When critical adults grew angry with

rambunctious children in the temple area, Jesus reminded them that it's "from the lips of children and infants" that God ordains praise (Matthew 21:16 NIV). Particularly when the praise is spontaneous.

How do we do that? How do we get ahold of the selfless contentment of children? How do we content ourselves when the commonalities of life bog us down in frustration and worry? Christ says to remember that God knows all about our daily needs. What we must do is "seek first his kingdom and his righteousness," and then "all these things will be given to [us] as well" (Matthew 6:33 NIV). (KAD)

GOD TURNS WEAKNESSES INTO STRENGTHS

*And he said unto me, My grace is sufficient
for thee: for my strength is made perfect in
weakness. Most gladly therefore will I rather
glory in my infirmities, that the power of Christ
may rest upon me. Therefore I take pleasure
in infirmities, in reproaches, in necessities, in
persecutions, in distresses for Christ's sake:
for when I am weak, then am I strong.*

2 CORINTHIANS 12:9-10 KJV

Fanny Crosby would no doubt agree with Paul's
words about his infirmities. Blinded when she
was six weeks old by a man posing as a doctor,
she never wasted a moment in anger or self-pity,
later writing, "I have not for a moment in more
than eighty-five years felt a spark of resentment
against him, because I have always believed that

the good Lord by this means consecrated me to the work that I am still permitted to do."

A gifted, prolific poet, Fanny was already well known for her readings and published poetry by the time she was accepted at the Institution for the Blind when she was fifteen. With a mind like quicksilver, she memorized great works of literature, including most of the Bible. She remained a student at the institute for twelve years, then was a teacher there for eleven. All the while her poetry circled the globe, and the young girl found that by eighteen she was receiving visits from presidents and dignitaries.

At twenty-three she stood before the US Congress, and at twenty-four she published her first book. But she was not yet a Christian. Fanny had loved the language of the Bible, but its message had never opened her heart. Finally, at thirty-one, she received the Lord in a revival meeting, describing her own conversion as a flash of "celestial light." God touched her mind and soul, and the floodgates opened.

Over the next sixty years, Fanny wrote more than eight thousand five hundred hymns, sometimes as many as seven a day! Inspiration came to her from everywhere, from ordinary sources, such as a carriage ride, to events that rocked her life, like the death of her infant daughter, for whom she wrote "Safe in the Arms of Jesus."

What Fanny could not see, she could feel, and God's love and blessings on her set aside her blindness in favor of a wisdom and a "sight" that few other people have experienced. Yet all of us can follow her example in finding the confidence to use what gifts God has bestowed on us, no matter what "infirmities" challenge our everyday lives. (RR)

FRIENDS BRING HAPPINESS

A friend loves at all times.

PROVERBS 17:17 NIV

*F*riends—television shows, hit songs, and countless stories have focused on the special people we call friends. Special occasions such as Friendship Week and Best Friend Day have even been established to honor them. Why? Because friends are important.

Friends are there for us in good times and bad. They support us when we need a shoulder to cry on. They encourage us when we need a boost of confidence. They celebrate with us when we accomplish our goals. They offer words of wisdom when we need advice. And, maybe most important, friends make life's journey a whole lot happier.

I can't imagine life without Raegan, Angie,

Susan, Barb, Gena, Camille, Karen, Steph, Sylvia, Jenny, and the other important gal pals in my life. They are the thread of joy that runs through my life. From conversations about who is the best singer on *American Idol* to yummy pancake breakfasts at Cracker Barrel to all-day shopping trips to aerobic workouts on Saturday mornings—the times I spend with my best buddies bring me much joy.

Do you have special friends in your life? If so, how long has it been since you have taken time to get together with them, phone them, or drop them a card to say hello? Friendships take work. They require a time investment on your part. But they are definitely worth the time and effort. If you don't have any close friends with whom you can share your life, ask God to send you some of those precious people. Or if you have been neglecting your friends, determine today to rekindle those relationships.

God didn't intend for us to go through life

alone. He knew we would need each other. He knew that friends would add a dimension of happiness to our lives that we wouldn't be able to get anywhere else. So celebrate your friends today—and enjoy the journey of life a little bit more. (MMA)

EDIBLE SERENITY

*Taste and see that the L*ORD *is good.*

PSALM 34:8 NIV

Try as I might, I can't find a single reference to chocolate in the Bible. Not a hint of cocoa or that sorry second, carob. The closest thing to chocolate in the Bible is honey—golden, stick-to-your-fingers honey. Golden chocolate, you might say. When we want a taste of edible delight, most of us reach for chocolate. I've yet to meet a woman who finds sweet consolation in a celery stick or a carrot. And let's be honest: an apple or an orange is just a guiltless substitution for the real thing.

No, when we girls want a serenely satisfying treat, we reach for the Snickers—or at least a shoe-size block of baklava. Oh, such sweet, heavenly savor. . . Sweet serenity for the soul is linked not to our taste buds but to God. The psalmist says

God's words to us are "sweeter than honey, than honey from the honeycomb" (Psalm 19:10 NIV). But sometimes the sweet pleasure of God's teaching can disagree with us. In the book of Revelation John says, "I took the little scroll from the angel's hand and ate it. It tasted as sweet as honey in my mouth, but when I had eaten it, my stomach turned sour" (Revelation 10:10 NIV). The whole counsel of God brings us both satisfying peace and hard-to-digest truth.

Jesus encouraged us to enjoy a soul feast of Him. "I am the bread of life. Whoever comes to me will never go hungry, and whoever believes in me will never be thirsty" (John 6:35 NIV). Not only is Jesus true soul food, but He is soul drink as well. "Whoever drinks the water I give them will never thirst. Indeed, the water I give them will become in them a spring of water welling up to eternal life" (John 4:14 NIV). Christ wraps up His shocking statements simply. "The one who feeds on me will live because of me. . . . Whoever

feeds on this bread [meaning Himself] will live forever" (John 6:57–58 NIV).

Need a sweet fix today? Need a serenity fix? The Lord invites us to feast on Him and His words. "How sweet are your words to my taste," exclaimed the psalmist; "Sweeter than honey to my mouth!" (Psalm 119:103 NIV). Find a spot and curl up with God's Word to start, end, or even get through the hump part of your day. Feast on the One who is the "true bread from heaven" (John 6:32)—and maybe grab a *small* handful of M&M's while you're at it. Very small. Very, very, very small. Then chow down on some spiritual and some physically edible serenity! (KAD)

GOD LOVES YOU—
FLAWS AND ALL

*So let's come near God with pure hearts and
a confidence that comes from having faith.*

HEBREWS 10:22 CEV

If you listen closely, you can hear them. Women around the globe, groaning and moaning in dressing rooms. Are they in pain? Are they ill? No, it's just bathing-suit season, and they're trying to find the one perfect suit that doesn't make them look fat. It's a quest every woman embarks on, and it's one of the most daunting tasks she will ever face.

Seriously, is there anything more humbling than standing in front of a dressing-room mirror, under those unforgiving fluorescent lights, trying on bathing suit after bathing suit? I think not. I dread it every year. Because no matter how many

miles you've logged in previous months, no matter how many crunches you've crunched, no matter how many desserts you've passed up, bathing suits show every imperfection.

While you might be able to hide a few dimples underneath blue jeans or a nice black dress, you're not hiding anything in a bathing suit. That's pretty much how it is with God. You might be able to fake-grin your way through church. You might be able to "play Christian" in front of your friends and family. But when you enter the throne room, it's like wearing your bathing suit before God. You can't hide any imperfections from Him. He sees it all.

That truth used to horrify me—even more than trying on bathing suits—but not anymore. Here's the great thing about God. He gave us Jesus to take care of our sin, because God knew we'd be flawed. No matter how many good deeds we do, no matter how many chapters of the Bible we read each day, and no matter how many casseroles we bake for church functions, we can never be good enough for God. We can't earn our way into God's favor. All we have to do is ask Jesus to be the Lord of our lives, and we're "in." Then, whenever we enter the throne room, God sees us through "the Jesus filter," and all He sees is perfection.

If you haven't asked Jesus to take away your sin and be the Lord of your life, why not take care of that today? It's the most wonderful step you'll ever make. Now if we could just figure out some kind of perfection filter for bathing-suit season, then life would be super. (MMA)

THE CONFIDENCE TO BE USED BY GOD

And Mary said: "My soul glorifies the Lord and my spirit rejoices in God my Savior, for he has been mindful of the humble state of his servant. From now on all generations will call me blessed."

LUKE 1:46-48 NIV

What if Mary had said no? She could have. God didn't make her accept His will for her life; He let her choose. As overwhelming as the appearance of an angel in her room must have been, Mary's choice should not have been an easy one. Her life was simple and stable: she was young, engaged to a good man, and ready to start her own home. Accepting God's will for her meant risking all of that and much more.

A woman who became pregnant during her

betrothal could be accused of adultery and stoned. At the very least, Joseph would know that the child was not his and break off his commitment to her. If she survived, her life would be ruined. Mary's mind, however, was on the Lord, not human society. She stood in awe of such an honor and asked only how God planned to achieve this miracle. When she sang her praises of the Lord later (see Luke 1:46–55), this young girl expressed her joy and pride in being chosen by God. Her love of God and understanding of scriptures gave her complete confidence in her unhesitant "Yes, Lord!"

Mary was indeed blessed, but being Jesus' mother also came with tremendous anxiety and heartache. She saw the glory of His miracles but also felt the pain of His death. Like any mother, she panicked when He went missing and rejoiced in His triumphs. And after His death, she joined His disciples in the upper room (see Acts 1:12–14) to pray, grieve, and be with those who loved Him.

Mary could have said no, the same as any

of us who feel God's tug on our lives. As Mary discovered, following God can lead us down a path filled with great pain as well as tremendous joy. Yet if we love Him and understand His love for us, then we will discover the confidence to say yes! (RR)

LET THE PAST BE
THE PAST AT LAST

*Forgetting what is behind and straining
toward what is ahead, I press on toward
the goal to win the prize for which God has
called me heavenward in Christ Jesus.*

PHILIPPIANS 3:13-14 NIV

Ralph Waldo Emerson wrote: "Finish each day and be done with it. You have done what you could; some blunders and absurdities have crept in; forget them as soon as you can. Tomorrow is a new day; you will begin it serenely and with too high a spirit to be encumbered with your old nonsense." In other words, "Get over it! Move on! Tomorrow is another day!" Okay, so you totally messed up yesterday. Maybe you yelled at your children, ate too many Twinkies, acted disrespectfully to your employer, or spoke sharply to your

spouse. Whatever you did wrong yesterday, be quick to repent and move on. The devil will try to make you dwell on your past mistakes, but you don't have to go there. Once you have asked for forgiveness—both from those people you offended and from Jesus Christ—you're good to go! You get to start the next day with a clean slate.

God doesn't remember the mistakes you have confessed, so why should you? Don't let yesterday's blunders steal today's joy. Remember, guilt and condemnation are not from the Father. So if you are experiencing those emotions, realize their origin—they come from the devil. He wants you to feel so bad about yourself that you will never move forward. Know why? Because the devil understands the awesome plans God has for your life, and he doesn't want you to enjoy your bright future. The enemy will do anything he can to keep you in your past, so don't fall for his tricks. Instead, learn from your mistakes and move on.

Let the past be the past at last! Praise the

Lord for His unending mercy and love, and ask Him to help you become more like Him. You are a work in progress. We are all like spiritual babies, learning to walk and occasionally falling down—and that's okay. Quit glancing back at your blunders; keep your eyes on Jesus. Your future is happy and bright in Him. (MMA)

GOD HAS CONFIDENCE
IN YOU

He delivered me from my strong enemy, and
from them which hated me: for they were too
strong for me. They prevented me in the day
of my calamity: but the LORD was my stay.
He brought me forth also into a large place;
he delivered me, because he delighted in me.

PSALM 18:17-19 KJV

How many times have your prayers been answered? How many times has God taken care of you? Your friends and family? What stressful situations have you passed through, trusting God to guide and protect you? How many times has it "worked out," when others thought it would not?

Perhaps you can think of an occasion when you trusted God to move actively in your life—the saving of a dear friend from disease, or perhaps a loved one's safe return home during a time of war, despite a life-threatening injury. Maybe it was during a difficult period in your youth, when confusion about where you "fit in" led to some ill-made choices for your life. At some point in our lives, our obstacles, our "calamities," may prevent us from living a godly life, from following the true path God has ordained for us. And yes, we may find it terrifying to acknowledge that we are overwhelmed. Yet if we trust in the Lord and give our lives over to Him, we can clearly see that "He brought me forth also into a large place; he delivered me, because he delighted in me" (Psalm 18:19 KJV).

Think about that! He delights in us! By believing in God's grace and love, by trusting Him in the face of any and all situations, we find confidence to deal with our troubles out of the infinite hope, strength, and ultimately wisdom that comes from loving the Lord. Nothing pleases God more than this, and by so doing we have acknowledged and allowed God's will and words into our hearts and minds. God knows your potential; He never gives up on you. He has confidence in the person you are right now and the person you can become. (RR)

STEP INTO YOUR DREAMS

God's Spirit doesn't make us slaves who are afraid of him. Instead, we become his children and call him our Father.

ROMANS 8:15 CEV

In the early 1950s, Lillian Vernon spent five hundred dollars on her first advertisement, offering monogrammed belts and handbags. That one little ad, that one little risk, produced a $32,000 profit! Today—more than fifty years later—Lillian Vernon is still selling gift items and personalized goodies through a very successful catalog sales program. In fact, her company now generates more than $250 million in sales every year. Now that's a lot of handbags!

She has quite a success story. But what if Lillian Vernon hadn't run that small ad? Back then, five hundred dollars was a lot of money to spend with no guarantee of recouping it. What if she hadn't taken that risk? Well, she wouldn't be a millionaire, and lots of folks would have to find another catalog to use for their annual Christmas shopping.

Maybe God has put a dream in your heart that is so big you haven't even shared it with anyone. Maybe God is directing you to take a risk in business or start your own Bible study or volunteer for your child's school or run for office. So what's stopping you? Why aren't you running that ad like Lillian Vernon? Why aren't you going for it?

If you're like most women, fear is holding you back. Fear is a very real emotion. It can get a grip on you that won't let go—until you make it let go through the Word of God. The Bible tells us that "God has not given us a spirit of fear" (2 Timothy 1:7 NLT). So if it didn't come from God, where did it come from? Satan, maybe? You bet. So get rid of that nasty old emotion.

Say out loud, "I can do all things through

Christ who strengthens me. I am the head and not the tail. I am more than a conqueror." Remind yourself of who you are in Christ Jesus on a daily basis. You are a child of the Most High King. You have the mind of Christ. God has crowned you with His favor. And those are just a few of the promises in His Word. So grab hold of God's promises, put fear behind you, and step into your dreams. Pretty soon, you'll be sharing your success story! (MMA)

FLEX THOSE MUSCLES!

Train yourself to be godly. For physical training is of some value, but godliness has value for all things, holding promise for both the present life and the life to come.

1 TIMOTHY 4:7-8 NIV

*F*or many of us a good workout brings a measure of balance to our lives. Whether it's aerobics, lifting, biking, or running, exercise is good for both our bodies and our heads. When we glide down a pristine slope in winter's snow or breathe deep of awakening spring during a toning walk, a sense of mental calm can overtake us even as our bodies glisten (men are the ones who *sweat*) and our hearts pump to keep the pace. We may not wear a satisfied smile on our faces while we firm it up and trim it down, but rumor has it we'll sleep better come bedtime.

For those of us who thrive on routine physical exercise, it's reassuring to know that God tells us our trek around the track isn't wasted time. "Of some value" in the Greek means exercise is useful, advantageous, profitable, and helpful. To study the letters of Paul the apostle is to meet a man who alludes to sports and physical exercise frequently. He compared himself spiritually to an athlete in training for the Greek games of his day—our modern-day Olympic games (see 1 Corinthians 9:24–27).

With all that said, the Bible takes us one step further. We may find focus and release in physical exercise. That's because physical exercise is good for us. "But godliness," we're also told, "has value for *all things*" (emphasis added). The kicker? We have to train ourselves to be godly. Excuse me? How in the world do we train ourselves in godliness? There's serenity in that?

We must "turn to God in repentance and have faith in our Lord Jesus" (Acts 20:21 NIV). We ask

God's forgiveness for our sin and disobedience against him. We trust in Christ who "died for our sins according to the Scriptures" and who "was raised on the third day according to the Scriptures" (1 Corinthians 15:3–4 NIV). As we then "continue to work out [our] salvation with fear and trembling. . .it is God who works in [us] to will and to act in order to fulfill his good purpose" (Philippians 2:12–13 NIV).

The final result brings a win-win situation for our spiritual and our physical well-being. "A heart at peace gives life to the body" (Proverbs 14:30 NIV). That's better than a two-hour marathon! (KAD)

WORMS AND ALL

*Not that I have already obtained all
this, or have already arrived at my goal,
but I press on to take hold of that for
which Christ Jesus took hold of me.*

PHILIPPIANS 3:12 NIV

*D*o you ever feel overwhelmed, as if you are about to be buried in the pile of mounting laundry in your hamper? Have you ever felt like everyone at work thinks you're a moron in a nice suit? Do you ever feel like twenty-four hours is simply not enough time to accomplish everything on your to-do list? There are times when I feel so overwhelmed and ill-equipped that I just want to run and hide under the bed. Then I think, *But God is God. He knew all of my shortcomings and faults before He entrusted me with all of these responsibilities, so He must see potential in me that I don't.*

Aren't you thankful that God looks at us through eyes of love instead of condemnation? On the days when I lose my temper with my family or fail to meet a work deadline or miss an opportunity to witness for Him simply because I'm too exhausted from the day-to-day burdens, I am immensely thankful that God is a patient, loving, always-seeing-the-best-in-me kind of God. I am not a perfect mother. I mess up at work sometimes. And I often bite off more than I can chew. But God is changing me and perfecting me from glory to glory. And He is doing the same for you!

He understands when we miss the mark. He cheers us on when we take a step closer to Him. He actually loves us even when we are at our very worst. Think about that for a moment. God loves us so much that He gave His only Son for us—in spite of our shortcomings and less-than-perfect moments.

So the next time you feel overwhelmed, less than worthy, and totally clueless—ask God to help you see yourself the way He sees you. He adores you. You're the apple of His eye—even if you are a bit wormy at times. Now that's something to be happy about! (MMA)

GET OVER IT!

Then Rachel said, "I have had a great
struggle with my sister, and I have won."
GENESIS 30:8 NIV

*O*ur ladies' Bible study group, studying Genesis, had come to the scripture portion about
Jacob and his dysfunctional family. The writer
of the study asked us to consider how we might
individually counsel sisters Rachel and Leah,
Jacob's competing wives. As women living in
another culture and thousands of years removed
from these two sisters, we each grappled with an
answer—except for one gal in our group. We all
wanted to hear what Cheryl, a Christian counselor
with years of experience, had to say.

Cheryl listened without comment to our
speculative answers. Thankfully, none of us has
ever had to share our husband's affection or

admiration with "sister wives." Our answers probably wouldn't have made a dent in the dynamics of this fractured family, but the question really made us think. What about Cheryl? What would be a professional Christian counselor's response to each sister? "I'd ask them both the same question," she said. That set all of us back. None of us had thought to pose a question first. "This is it: 'How is this competition helping you achieve your goal?'"

Whoa. Unloved wife Leah, doing what increased her stature and Jacob's in their culture (having lots of boy babies), wanted her husband's love. Childless Rachel, loved adoringly by Jacob, wanted to have his children. Each woman took out her frustration on her sister. Neither found contentment in what she had. They only found frustration in what they lacked. But how was their competition helping Rachel conceive? How was it aiding Leah in her desire to win her husband's heart?

Are you giving yourself to a competition that won't help you achieve your goal? Do you allow situations over which you have no control to drag you into a cycle of frustration, anger, or self-pity? The Bible never tells us if Rachel and Leah were able to get beyond their competition to a place of contentment. But the question remains for us to answer if some rivalry holds our serenity at bay. A sincere prayer to the God who can give us real contentment may get us started. Try paraphrasing 2 Thessalonians 3:16. "Lord of peace, please give me your peace no matter what happens." (KAD)

A SELFLESS VESSEL

Love is patient and kind. Love is
not jealous or boastful or proud.

1 CORINTHIANS 13:4 NLT

My neighbor Melanie is definitely a dog lover. She and her husband have two "little boys"—Rupert and Jackson. They are the most adorable little fluff balls you've ever seen. And let me tell you, these puppies are treated like royalty. I often meet the couple taking "the boys" on their evening jaunt, and we'll chat about our precious puppies. (I have three adorable miniature long-haired dachshunds.)

Not long ago, Melanie told me that she had decided to adopt a little girl dog to join in the fun. She had seen a Humane Society advertisement in the local paper, and this little poodle mix named Peaches had captured Mel's heart. She went on to say, "I couldn't bear the thought of this little poodle being put down." So Mel adopted Peaches and took her to the veterinarian for all of her necessary shots.

As it turned out, Peaches had a bad case of kennel cough, so Mel had to leave her at the vet's for a week or so. But every single day, Mel would go to the vet's office and play with Peaches, petting her and talking nice to her. She wanted Peaches to know she would be loved at her new home. The two bonded.

On the day that Mel was supposed to bring Peaches home, she overheard the veterinarian talking to a woman who was looking for a dog to be a companion for her elderly father. He lived in a retirement home, and his beloved cocker spaniel had recently passed away, leaving him very lonely and depressed.

As Mel listened to the woman's story, she knew what she had to do. Peaches was needed somewhere else—even though Mel already loved that little poodle as if she'd owned her for years. As the delighted and grateful woman left the veterinarian's office with Peaches under her arm, Mel sobbed. But she wasn't crying because she was sad. She was crying tears of joy because she knew God had truly used her that day.

She had been the selfless vessel He needed to make an old man's dream come true. A selfless heart is a rare and beautiful thing today, but you can always spot the ones who have such hearts. They seem to glow with goodness. So have you done any selfless acts lately? Are you available to be that selfless vessel for God? In this dog-eat-dog world, God needs us to glow with goodness. Be a selfless vessel today. (MMA)

THE CONFIDENCE TO FOLLOW CHRIST UNCEASINGLY

Early on Sunday morning, while it was still dark, Mary Magdalene came to the tomb and found that the stone had been rolled away from the entrance.

JOHN 20:1 NLT

M ary couldn't wait. Her unwavering loyalty to Christ continued, even though He had died on the cross. She arose well before dawn and went to His grave to anoint His body with burial spices (see Mark 16:1), as one last task she could do for her Lord. Her discovery of the open tomb led to astonishment and grief, as she assumed the Romans had taken Him away. She ran to tell Peter and the "other disciple, whom Jesus loved" (John 20:2 KJV), and they too saw that His body was gone, but they simply returned to their homes. Mary waited.

Throughout the New Testament, while most of those around Jesus doubted, denied, or fled, Mary and some of the other women stayed by His side. They traveled with the disciples during good times, and they helped support Jesus' ministry financially (see Luke 8:1–3). Mary's devotion began the moment He freed her from seven demons, and she didn't abandon Him or her faith when His journey turned toward the crucifixion. She was not afraid of being associated with Jesus, and she followed him up to Golgotha and down again to the tomb. The reward for this devotion came as she waited by the empty tomb, weeping.

Spotting a man she thought was the gardener, she begged for information about Jesus. Instead, she heard the voice she thought was gone forever. " 'Sir,' she said, 'if you have taken him away, tell me where you have put him, and I will go and get him.' 'Mary!' Jesus said. She turned to him and cried out, 'Rabboni!' " (John 20:15–16 NLT).

Mary Magdalene was the first person to see Jesus after His resurrection, the first to know that the prophecies were true, the first to discover that Christ was alive forever. Rejoicing, she ran to tell others of the good news. Mary's loyalty reminds us that devoting our lives to the Lord isn't always simple. Allegiance to God takes determination as well as love.

Many times, believers will lose the intensity they felt after their conversion, or they'll devote prayer time to Him only when they need something. Giving ourselves to Him, however, is the least we can do for the One who gave Himself so totally to us. (RR)

SPREAD THE JOY!

Love is kind.

1 CORINTHIANS 13:4 NIV

*E*very single day we encounter joy stealers. You know the type—rude cashiers, angry drivers, inconsiderate coworkers, and even grouchy family members. You'll have an opportunity (probably before breakfast) to get mad, but you can choose kindness instead. Not long ago I encountered one of those joy stealers at the supermarket.

This cashier was angry. I don't know why—maybe she'd had a fight with her husband before work, or maybe her boss had just given her crummy hours for the next week. Whatever the cause, this gal was not in a good mood. As she scanned my items, she was muttering under her breath. Though I hated to disturb her, I had a few coupons to use, which I slid toward her. Glaring

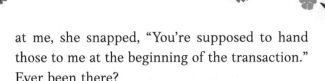

at me, she snapped, "You're supposed to hand those to me at the beginning of the transaction." Ever been there?

Now, what I wanted to say was, "Listen, sister, I'll report your rudeness to your supervisor. Don't push me." But my heart wouldn't let me. Instead, I answered, "Oh, I'm sorry. I wasn't aware of that policy. If it's too much trouble, I can just save them and use them the next time I go grocery shopping." She didn't even respond, so I continued. "I bet you get tired of rule breakers like me, eh?"

She cracked a smile. "Some days it's an aggravating job," she shared in a much nicer tone.

"Well, I don't envy you," I added. "I used to work retail for a clothing store, and I know how the public can be. Some days I just wanted to scream."

"You've got that right," she chimed in.

Before she scanned my last can of green beans, we were best buddies. She not only let me use my coupons but she gave me a couple of extra ones she had at her station. We chatted a bit more while she bagged my groceries, and then I told her to keep up the good work and try not to let the aggravation get to her. She smiled a full-out smile and said, "I'll try not to. . .and you come back and see me."

I didn't let this cashier steal my joy. Instead, I gave her some of mine. You can do the same. Joy is contagious. Be a carrier and spread it everywhere you go. (MMA)

GOD IS THE SOURCE OF YOUR STRENGTH

My health may fail, and my spirit may
grow weak, but God remains the strength
of my heart; he is mine forever.

PSALM 73:26 NLT

Susanna Wesley is the perfect example of how influential a mother can be on not only her children but the world at large. Anyone intimidated by the "good wife" of Proverbs 31 should take a second look at Susanna, whose life can make most of us weak in the knees.

Born in 1669, Susanna was one of twenty-five children born to Samuel Annesley, a minister who filled his house with a broad range of people, some of them famous men of politics and academia. The lively—and crowded—household was filled with debate and dissent, and curious Susanna took it all in, learning Greek, Hebrew, theology, and literature from her father and his friends.

In 1688 she married Samuel Wesley, a young Church of England minister. The marriage was fruitful, if not particularly happy. The first nineteen years of her marriage Susanna gave birth to nineteen children, although nine of them died while still infants. Her home burned twice, once almost taking five-year-old John with it. Her grief, multiple births, and poor living conditions left the young woman ill much of the time, but Susanna didn't give up or dwell on her hardships.

With money tight and her husband often gone, Susanna grew even more determined to give her children the kind of education and home life she had growing up. So began her Sunday evening meetings. In addition to the standard lessons she gave the children, these discussions centered around scripture reading and the sermons they had heard that morning. They were intended just for family, but word soon spread, and before long a crowd started showing up.

At a time when most women weren't allowed to speak in church, much less from the pulpit, Susanna Wesley found the strength and confidence to speak to more than two hundred people every week. The profound impact her determination had on her children cannot be denied. Charles wrote more than eighteen hundred hymns, and her son John went on to change the face of Christianity. While Susanna's health was frequently weak, her strength and confidence came from the One who never fails. (RR)

HAPPINESS IS A
BEAUTIFUL THING

A happy heart makes the face cheerful. . . .
The cheerful heart has a continual feast.

PROVERBS 15:13, 15 NIV

My mother has always been a happy person. It didn't matter if it was raining outside. It didn't matter if our air-conditioning went out in mid-July. It didn't matter if one of her friends talked ugly to her. Mom has always chosen happiness. Growing up, Mom's happiness bugged me. She'd begin each day something like this. She'd burst into my bedroom, flip on my light switch, and begin her very loud rendition of "This is the day that the Lord has made. Let us rejoice and be glad in it." She'd sing at the top of her lungs and occasionally clap in time, as well. What a way to start the day, eh? There was no sleeping in at our house, because if you didn't get up, she'd

just start another verse!

After my father passed away last year, I didn't hear my mom singing anymore. I worried about her. I prayed to God, "Please restore the song back into my mother's life." After a period of grieving, little by little, I saw Mom's happiness return. It started with a hum, and now she's all-out singing again. I'm still waiting for that loud clapping to return, but I'm sure it's in the works. Why? Because Mom doesn't base her happiness on her circumstances. Sure, she's lonely without Daddy, but she chooses to be happy because of Jesus. She chooses to focus on the beauty in life—not the tragedy.

How is your happiness level? If it has been a while since you've burst forth in song, give it a whirl! Sing praises unto God until you sing yourself happy. But you say, "Michelle, you don't know what I'm going through right now. There's no way I can be happy." You may be right. But through Jesus you *can* be happy. Job 8:21 says, "He will yet fill your mouth with laughter and your lips with shouts of joy" (NIV). That's a promise you can count on! He will—but you have to want it.

You have to choose happiness. Comedy writer Robert Orben once said, "Happiness is contagious. Be a carrier!" That's pretty good advice. If you choose to be happy, you'll discover more people will want to be around you. Being happy simply makes you more attractive. Your happiness will be infectious. Happiness will become a lifelong habit, as it has been for my mom. You may even find yourself humming happily all day long. Beware: loud clapping is soon to follow! Go ahead—choose happiness today! It's a beautiful life! (MMA)

THE CONFIDENCE TO LEAD

*He [Apollos] began to speak boldly in
the synagogue. When Priscilla and
Aquila heard him, they invited him
to their home and explained to him
the way of God more adequately.*

ACTS 18:26 NIV

*P*riscilla and her husband, Aquila, may have
been the world's first husband and wife
ministry team. They certainly set a standard for
leadership, and Priscilla's equal partnership with
Aquila stands as a reminder that God gives women
ministerial gifts to use and reach others for Christ.

Priscilla and Aquila left Rome when the emperor
Claudius expelled all the Jews. They settled in
Corinth and established a tent-making business,
working together. When Paul came to Corinth
in AD 50, he stayed with them, working alongside

them, since he too was a tentmaker by trade.

This gave them an extraordinary opportunity to learn the Gospel message, to question Paul, and to absorb the intricacies of Jesus' teachings. For the next eighteen months, the three of them worked to build the church in Corinth, and when Paul left, Priscilla and Aquila went with him as far as Ephesus. These two were very influential in Ephesus, remaining after Paul left in order to teach and build a foundation for the believers there. They ran a house church (see 1 Corinthians 16:19), and in one of the most profound examples of their work, they watched the dynamic speaker Apollos and recognized not only his gifts but also the errors in his message.

Instead of confronting him, however, they took him aside privately, offering him correction and encouragement (see Acts 18:26). Their goal was to strengthen the body of Christ, not humiliate someone making mistakes. They remained staunch friends with Paul, however, who continued to greet them in his letters even after they returned to Rome (see 2 Timothy 4:19).

Scholars have sometimes pointed to the fact that Priscilla is mentioned first and as often as Aquila as evidence that Paul sees them as partners, equal in strength. Larry Richards, in his in-depth book *Every Woman in the Bible,* reflects on the creation of woman in Genesis and suggests, "In Priscilla and Aquila we see the transformation of marriage and the restoration of God's original intent that married couples should be partners in all things in their life."

Without a doubt, Priscilla and Aquila helped transform the early church, despite exile, threat of death (see Romans 16:4), and the need to make a living. Women can still look to Priscilla to see that they definitely should have the confidence to minister to others when the need arises. (RR)

WHAT WAS HER SECRET?

*"And who knows but that you have come to
your royal position for such a time as this?"*

ESTHER 4:14 NIV

Hadassah's story makes for a great read, but living it probably gave the young woman who became Queen Esther, wife of King Xerxes, more than one stress headache and nervous stomach. Hadassah, a Jewish girl also known as Esther, had been selected to replace Queen Vashti. Vashti had refused her husband's request to parade herself before his friends and associates. A search was made for an acceptable replacement for Vashti, and Esther was taken from her home as the "winner."

Esther transitions from simple Jewish girl to queen of Persia and Media. She goes from rags to riches, from no cosmetics to a full year of intensive spa treatments. (Check out Esther 2:12–14.)

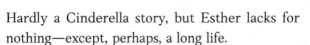

Hardly a Cinderella story, but Esther lacks for nothing—except, perhaps, a long life.

An adviser to the king persuades Xerxes to wipe out every Jew in the empire. When Esther learns of the decree through the cousin who raised her, he gives her some chilling words. "Do not think that because you are in the king's house you alone of all the Jews will escape" (Esther 4:13 NIV). If Esther had any composure left after being taken from her home and then relegated to a place in the harem apart from her initially doting (but now apparently indifferent) husband, this no doubt ended it.

Yet Esther presents herself in the account as a woman confidently—and possibly serenely— handling her impending doom with unhurried grace and that most womanly wile of all: willing submission to her man (see Esther 5:1–8). Esther may have been a bundle of nerves when she approached her king without his summons. Yet it's unlikely Xerxes would have welcomed a whimpering wife into his presence.

He knew and she knew that to go to the king without being asked meant her death—unless he extended his scepter to her. But even after Xerxes does just that, Esther carefully executes each step of her plan to prevent the promised genocide. Queen Esther successfully delivers her people from sure destruction. She once again gains the favor of her husband, the king. How she does it is recorded in chapters 5 through 9.

But the secret of her poise, the activity that preceded her actions, may surprise you. It's not so much what she does as what she doesn't do. Her secret is found in Esther 4:15–16. It's a secret worth investigating. (KAD)

DRIVE YOUR WAY
TO HAPPINESS

*Jesus answered, "It is written: 'Man shall
not live on bread alone, but on every word
that comes from the mouth of God.'"*

MATTHEW 4:4 NIV

Today's pace is insanely fast, isn't it? We go, go, go—all the time. We drive to and from work; to and from school; to and from the health club; to and from soccer practice, gymnastics class, dance class, (fill in the blank) class; to and from dental and doctor appointments; to and from the grocery store, dry cleaner, and other places of business; to and from our children's games and events; and on and on it continues. Sometimes I feel like I spend more time in my SUV than I do at home. Actually, if I added up the minutes, I probably do spend more time behind the wheel than at home.

From where I live in Fort Worth, everything is about twenty-five minutes away, so I'm forced to drive a large percentage of every single day. I used to sit in traffic and stress over things in my life. I'd drive like a maniac, trying to make my next appointment on time and occasionally bordering on road rage. I discovered that all that driving was literally driving me crazy, so I decided to make better use of the time.

Much to my tween-age daughters' disdain, I began turning off the car radio and tuning in to God. Sometimes I play praise and worship CDs. At other times I listen to teachings from my favorite preachers. Some days I listen to the Bible on CD. On still other days I use those minutes to commune with the Master. I pray out loud for everyone on my prayer list and spend time praising the Lord for everything good in my life.

Now when I arrive at my destination, I'm not a stressed-out mess. Instead, I'm refueled with the love of God, fresh insights into His Word, and a renewed sense of happiness. I always joke that I have the most sanctified SUV in all of Texas. How sanctified is your vehicle? Some people call it "multitasking" when you accomplish more than one thing at a time. I just call it "keeping my sanity in the midst of a crazy, stressed-out life." Don't dread your drive time anymore. Instead, use that time to draw closer to God. Happy trails! (MMA)

CONTRIBUTORS

Michelle Medlock Adams (MMA) has a diverse résumé featuring inspirational books, children's picture books, and greeting cards. Her insights have appeared in periodicals across America, including *Today's Christian Woman* and *Guideposts for Kids*. She lives in Fort Worth, Texas, with her husband, two daughters, and a "mini petting zoo."

Katherine Anne Douglas (KAD) has authored numerous articles and books, and she has contributed to several anthologies. She enjoys leading women's Bible studies at her church. Kathy and her husband live in Fulton County, Ohio.

Ramona Richards (RR), an award-winning writer, editor, and speaker, is the fiction editor for Abingdon Press. She's the author of nine books and is a frequent contributor to devotional collections, including *Secrets of Confidence, Heavenly Humor for the Woman's Soul,* and *Heavenly Humor for the Dieter's Soul.* An avid live-music fan, Ramona loves her adopted hometown of Nashville, Tennessee.